FINANCIAL FREEDOM

A GUIDE TO ACHIEVING LIFELONG WEALTH AND SECURITY

Reuben Advani

Financial Freedom: A Guide to Achieving Lifelong Wealth and Security

ISBN-13 (pbk): 978-1-4302-4539-1

ISBN-13 (electronic): 978-1-4302-4540-7

Trademarked names may appear in this book. Rather than use a trademark symbol with every occurrence of a trademarked name, we use the names only in an editorial fashion and to the benefit of the trademark owner, with no intention of infringement of the trademark.

President and Publisher: Paul Manning
Acquisitions Editor: Morgan Ertel
Editorial Board: Steve Anglin, Mark Beckner, Ewan Buckingham, Gary Cornell, Louise Corrigan, Morgan Ertel, Jonathan Gennick, Jonathan Hassell, Robert Hutchinson, Michelle Lowman, James Markham, Matthew Moodie, Jeff Olson, Jeffrey Pepper, Douglas Pundick, Ben Renow-Clarke, Dominic Shakeshaft, Gwenan Spearing, Matt Wade, Tom Welsh
Coordinating Editor: Rita Fernando
Copy Editor: Ann Dickson
Compositor: Bytheway Publishing Services
Indexer: SPi Global
Cover Designer: Anna Ishchenko

Distributed to the book trade worldwide by Springer-Verlag New York, Inc., 233 Spring Street, 6th Floor, New York, NY 10013. Phone 1-800-SPRINGER, fax 201-348-4505, e-mail orders-ny@springer-sbm.com, or visit www.springeronline.com.

For information on translations, please contact us by e-mail at info@apress.com, or visit www.apress.com.

Apress and friends of ED books may be purchased in bulk for academic, corporate, or promotional use. eBook versions and licenses are also available for most titles. For more information, reference our Special Bulk Sales–eBook Licensing web page at www.apress.com/bulk-sales. To place an order, email your request to support@apress.com

To my sister, Ramona Advani, for showing me that anyone can master the art of personal finance.

Contents

About the Author

Reuben Advani is the founder and president of Telestrat Education, a continuing education company that specializes in business skills training through online and in-person instruction. Mr. Advani began his career with Morgan Stanley & Co., Inc., where he worked in the firm's corporate finance division. In this capacity, he performed detailed valuation analysis of acquisition targets for Fortune 500 companies and oversaw the coordination of several debt and equity issuances. His next position was with Sony Corporation of America, where he was active in the development of Sony's online initiatives. Mr. Advani has provided consulting services to companies throughout the United States and Latin America and has held interim positions, including CFO and COO, at several of them. He is a frequent speaker on topics ranging from corporate valuation to financial reporting and has addressed audiences across the United States, Europe, and Asia. Mr. Advani is the author of the popular business book, *The Wall Street MBA*, holds a B.A. from Yale University, an M.B.A. from The Wharton School, and has taught university-level finance.

Acknowledgments

Many people helped make this book possible. I want to thank my mom, Dolly Advani, who is a constant source of support, and my sister, Ramona Advani, who offers her help to those in need (which is usually me). My talented colleague, Alexis DeRemigi, always delivers exceptional results which makes my job easier. I want to thank Morgan Ertel at Apress for believing in me on more than one occasion and helped shape this book. I owe a great deal of gratitude to Jeffrey Pepper and Rita Fernando at Apress who helped bring my book to completion.

Several people have offered me guidance over the last several years and I believe I would not be where I am today without their help. Robert Borghese and Fred Lipman are always willing to offer valuable advice whenever needed and I appreciate their help. I want to thank Rakesh Jain, Sajjad Jaffer, Maziar Akram, and Vikram Sodhi. They form my de facto financial brain trust. Two individuals helped me start my career in finance, Adam and Richard Pechter, and I owe a special thanks to them. I would like to extend thanks to Gary Podorowsky and Nick Henny who taught me the business side of finance and to Steve Fredette for believing in the value of a financial education.

I would also like to thank my friend Dr. Ravi Goel for teaching me that even non-finance types can appreciate finance. Shom Chowdhury and Nimitt Mankad are strong supporters of everything I do so I want to extend a special thanks to them (plus, I know I will sell at least two copies of this book because of them). My deepest gratitude is offered to Tomer Rothshild and Matt Zaklad for their philosophical approach to finance and other worldly pursuits and to Eric Gehl for his tremendous insights on real estate matters.

Many thanks are owed to my friends Brian Buck, Mike Siegel, Oriol Sunyer and Ignacio Delgado who keep me smiling during stressful times. Finally, I owe special thanks to my daughter and future boss, Leena, who likes to keep her dad on task.

Introduction

At the onset of my midlife crisis, I decided to respond aggressively to the symptoms of aging by doing what any rational person would do: I took up paragliding. My first launch did not go as planned. After rising about 40 feet in what seemed like a few seconds, I quickly fell to the ground just as fast. As I lay in a dusty cornfield with the wind knocked out of me and unable to move my neck, two thoughts entered my mind: 1.) I hope I'm dead which is presumably less painful than what I'm about to feel if I'm not and 2.) I need to write a personal finance book. Well, as you can imagine, the hope expressed in my first thought was not recognized and the desire to write a personal finance book became a reality. One out of two ain't bad.

What went wrong with my foray into paragliding? For starters, poor preparation. My training consisted of two minutes of instruction while strapped to a beam in a barn. Hardly enough to master the art of flight. Second, I maintained an overriding presumption that everything would work out for the best. Wrong again. It was this clear lack of rational thinking that landed me flat on my back. Finally, I clung to the belief that no matter what, I would be flying high soon. I looked around and saw my compatriots vaulting skyward and simply assumed I would be next. In the end, I realized that paragliding is not unlike personal finance. Too many of us fail to train properly for the financial rigors of life. Too many of us assume that everything will work out. Too many of us assume that we will achieve the financial success of those around us.

Why a personal finance book? This has become something of an obsession of mine for quite some time. As you may know, several years ago I penned the now famous tome (at least my mom thinks it's famous) *The Wall Street MBA*. The idea was to bring the world of business finance and accounting to the masses. After several years in the financial world, I realized that very few people actually understood finance and decided it was time to decode the mysteries of this realm. Over the years, the book has developed a strong following and was revised recently to include new chapters. I'm proud of the book but have always felt that business finance is one thing, personal finance another. Clearly, overlapping themes abound but overall, personal finance is a unique animal and one that has never been properly explained. This is my attempt.

I present to you *Financial Freedom*. My hope is that everyone across the globe grabs a copy of it. And on your book shelf, nestled between *Ulysses* and *Moby Dick* ... sits your copy of *Financial Freedom*. Okay, that might be a bit much. Perhaps a more realistic goal is that you read the book, in parts or in its entirety, and develop a solid understanding of how to manage most aspects of your financial life. Mastering the realm of personal finance will not guarantee your happiness, but it can certainly eliminate a lot of worry. More importantly, it can create opportunities that just might create happiness. In essence, consider this a major aspect of personal enhancement and more importantly, an integral part of leading the best life possible. So read the book, leave your financial worries behind, and get the most out of your life. Or, just buy the book and display it proudly on your shelf.

Assets

Balance Your Balance Sheet, Part I

Nobody likes going to the doctor and for good reason. The best-case scenario is that you spend the majority of your day anxiously waiting for someone to tell you that you're in good health but you need to take better care of yourself, watch what you eat, and get plenty of rest. The worst-case scenario … well, need I say more? But, what if you could eliminate all the anxiety associated with this potential ordeal? What if your doctor's report was available to you at all times allowing you to determine your health status at any moment? The result of any health decision could then be predetermined. Want that second cheeseburger? No problem because my doctor's report won't reveal any problems. How about fries with it? Go for it! Unfortunately, life and, more importantly, nature are not that simple. However, when it comes to your financial health, simplicity just might be possible. To achieve this, let's discuss the wonders of the balance sheet because understanding one will help you understand your own financial health.

Corporations live and die by their balance sheets, which offer key insights into their financial health. While most corporations will have a chief financial officer (CFO) who spends days and nights agonizing over the corporate balance sheet, in personal finance you have to become your own personal CFO. In other words, your life is one big, complex corporation and you have to treat it with care in order to ensure its continued success. To do that, you have to actively manage your own balance sheet. And if you do this effectively, you just might gain a better sense of your financial health and, in turn, make the best decisions for your financial future.

The balance sheet helps you understand what you have, what you owe, and, ultimately, what you are worth. Understanding these three areas is the first step in assessing your financial health. Just as your doctor carefully checks your heart when you go in for a checkup, your finances deserve to be evaluated with the same care. Enough said. This chapter will focus on assets, the first part of the balance sheet, and cover the following topics:

- What are assets?
- Listing and valuing assets
- Appreciable assets
- Depreciable assets
- It's assets that make the world go 'round

What Are Assets?

In the business world, an asset is a store of value and one that creates benefit for the company. It's something the business possesses and deploys to create some future benefit. Cash, inventory, property, plant, and equipment are all considered business assets because they have value and can create benefit for the business. In personal finance, an asset represents anything you can assign value to. Clearly, this definition can be broad based. My Pink Floyd *Dark Side of the Moon* T-shirt is arguably worth more to me than my car, but the market doesn't necessarily see it that way. In personal finance, determining your asset value is assessing what the market is willing to pay for it. When it comes to personal assets, we have a tendency to assign high value to things that create some level of utility for us personally. This, however, does not always equate with financial gain. Although these items might create some level of fulfillment, they do not help create a personal balance sheet. That amazing pet rock, potato chip resembling your favorite movie star, or sand from your first spring-break trip may carry personal significance but will not help you build a strong personal balance sheet. This is why it's important to only consider items for which there is a justifiable market value.

Listing and Valuing Assets

Listing and valuing your assets is an important step in assessing your financial health. Creating a list of assets involves a simple test that begs the question "What would someone pay for this?" Assuming there is some sort of resale value for each item is the tough part, but who said this would be easy? When it comes to personal finance, the best thing to do is take a page out of the groundbreaking book *The Wall Street MBA* (page 32 to be exact) and mark-to-market your asset values. In other words, if you can find market values for something, you can pinpoint its value. This can be relatively easy when it comes to liquid assets such as cash. You simply check your bank account and the cash balance listed is the cash value. But when it comes to other items such as homes, cars, and jewelry, things can get a bit more complicated. For the average person, these assets would include the following:

- Home
- Car
- Investment portfolio
- Retirement plan
- Home furnishings
- Investment real estate
- Artwork
- Jewelry
- Other

Determining values for each item can be a challenge so the best you can do is estimate.

Cash

Let's start with the basics. Cash is something we all have or at least we hope to have. On a personal balance sheet, cash would be one of the first items to list. Consider the cash in your bank account. Perhaps you have several bank accounts, in which case you will need to make a list. This will include checking, savings, and money market accounts. List each account including the bank name, account number, and current cash balance. This will not only help you determine how much cash you have, but it will help you get organized.

Securities

Stocks, bonds, options—oh, my! Securities can be confusing, especially given that nowadays you may have more items on this list than you care to remember, many of which you don't even understand. Not to worry. Help is on the way in later chapters. For now, make a list of each brokerage account and the value stated from your most recent monthly statement. If you're really ambitious, find the real-time value by logging on to your online account and checking the most recent balance.

Home

If you own a home, its value will be a big part of the asset section of your balance sheet. Home prices are often difficult to peg and, as such, valuing your home could prove challenging. When the housing market is weak, this task can be next to impossible. The best thing you can do is look for comparable home values based on what your neighbors are selling their houses for. When banks value your home as part of the mortgage application process, they will often hire an appraiser who will conduct a series of valuation exercises to determine the property's value. The appraiser will look at comparable home values in the neighborhood, run a fancy financial model, and ultimately guess what the value is. Appraisals can be pricey and are far from perfect so it probably would not be in your best interest to spend time and money on one unless required. You could, on the other hand, compare properties for sale in your area and look at the offer price or, better yet, recent sale amounts. Of course, no two properties are alike so you will likely need to consider average price per square foot. Yes, there is some math here.

Sale Price	Square Footage	Price/Square Foot
$ 330,000	3,000	$ 110
$ 440,000	4,400	$ 100
$ 240,000	2,000	$ 120
$ 340,000	3,400	$ 100
	Ave. Price/Sq. Ft. $	107.50
1,600 sq. ft X $ 107.500	$	172,000

Figure 1-1. Do-it-yourself home appraisal

In Figure 1-1, four properties are listed. For each one, a price per square foot is listed based on recent home sales which allows you to calculate an average price per square foot for the neighborhood. (Hint: It works out to $107.50.) If your home has 1,600 square feet, an appropriate market value would be calculated in the following way:

$107.50/sq. ft. x 1,600 sq. ft. = $172,000

This may not be the price you would receive if you sold your property today, but it's a decent estimate and good enough for purposes of assessing your home value.

Furniture

Furniture rarely provides much value, but take the quiz below anyway to determine if you should value your furniture:

1.   Does your living room look like the setting for an E.M. Forster novel?

2. Do you call your living room "the parlor"?

3. Do you sleep under a mosquito net?

4. Do you sip tea with your pinky finger extended?

If you answered yes to any of these questions, your furniture just might have some reasonable market value. Otherwise, used furniture has very little resale value. If you're eager to pin a value on your couch, ottoman, armoire, canopy bed, and so forth, your best bet is to check for similar items and their prices at your local Goodwill. Don't expect much.

Artwork

Own any expensive works of art? Have any idea what someone might pay for them? If you answered yes to both questions, it's worth making a list of these pieces and estimating their value. In other words, guess. If Junior's finger painting on the refrigerator door is your home's *Mona Lisa*, please skip this section.

Car

In the twenty-first century, cars have become a major part of our lives. And while we can debate whether or not a car is financially beneficial, the bottom line is that a car has value and should be noted on your personal balance sheet. Determining the value can be tough, but the blue book value is a good starting point. You can visit http://www.kbb.com/ online to get a pretty good assessment.

There you have it. The bulk of personal assets will fall into these categories. In the example below, we'll take a look at a sample personal balance sheet. Our friend, Tony, moved to the United States a few years ago and started an import-export business. He seems to be doing more importing than exporting, and business is booming. He recently married and is building a terrific life for himself in South Florida. Take a look at his personal assets:

Tony's Assets		
Cash	2	million
Miami Mansion	5	million
Petting Zoo	1	million
Wife's Jewelry	1	million
Cars	1	million
Boats	2	million
Furniture (including custom-made fountain)	1	million
Stock (shares in various Colombian-based commodities companies)	8	million
Total Assets	**21**	**million**

Figure I-2. Tony's assets

Tony's assets, shown in Figure I-2, seem to be well diversified, forming a nice mix of what we'll discuss next: appreciable and depreciable assets.

Appreciable Assets

There is a reason why celebrities have multiple homes. Sure, they could afford to stay in the finest hotels in the world, but having homes in New York, Palm Springs, and Gstaad affords them bragging rights as well as an opportunity to recognize some healthy gains when real estate prices increase. The financial crisis of 2008–2011 taught us that real estate prices do not always increase. However, the hope is that over a long enough period of time, price appreciation should be the norm. So, why not take a lesson out of the pages of the celebrity investment handbook and buy property? For starters, multiple home purchases are not something most of us can afford. Nonetheless, the point is well taken. It's probably better to buy homes than clothes, cars, or anything else that loses value. When it comes to buying assets, your bias should be towards appreciable ones, which include these items:

- Real Estate
- Securities
- Artwork
- Jewelry

Depreciable Assets

Who doesn't like nice things? Cars, homes, clothes, and so forth. Living well is feeling well, right? Not always, but nice things can sure create some nice feelings. Whether you choose to live like MC Hammer or Gandhi, the choice is yours and what you buy will make all the difference. If you want to live like a millionaire, you need to be one. Make certain your asset purchases reflect your financial goals. Not all assets will fulfill this goal, but it helps to be aware of those that will. Some assets will continue to lose value over their expected life and ultimately prove detrimental to your financial goals. Cars, boats, furniture, and computers are all highly depreciable assets. With the passage of time, they are worth less. Just because they lose value, however, doesn't mean you shouldn't own them. Some are necessary and others are just a whole lot of fun. But too much of a good thing can be bad, so make certain your asset base is not disproportionately weighted towards depreciable assets. In other words, that boat might seem like a good idea but a stock portfolio might serve your financial interests better. Or, if you must invest in fun, consider the vacation home versus the houseboat.

Depreciable Assets

- Clothes
- Furniture
- Cars
- Boats
- Planes

Why Depreciable Assets Are Good

- They're fun.
- We need them.

Why Depreciable Assets Are Bad

- They lose value.
- They can cost money to maintain.

It's Assets That Make the World Go 'Round

As an armchair movie critic, I rank the Oscar winning classic *Out of Africa* in my top-ten list. As an author of finance books, I can honestly say Robert Redford's character, Denys, leaves something to be desired. Sure, he's dashing, confident, and adventurous, but his disdain for possessing assets runs against the grain of this book. He prefers the simple life and repeatedly shuns the Western tendency to build one's asset base. So, unless you plan on living the nomadic life in sub-Saharan Africa, please disregard this character's repeated criticisms of his love interest's buildup of personal assets.

Chapter Lessons

- Build your assets. It rarely hurts to build your asset base and, as we've discussed, assets improve your financial health.

- Purchase more appreciable assets than depreciable ones. It's simple. If your asset purchase is likely to increase in value over time, it probably makes sense. That's not to say that depreciable assets should be avoided at all costs. In some cases, they can be necessities and, in others, they're just plain fun. Just be careful not to spend your hard-earned money on things that will be worth next to nothing in a few years.

- Make your assets work for you. Ultimately, your assets should work for you. Think of your assets as a hiring decision and each one you purchase will ultimately become a hardworking employee. Make the right choice and you will see solid results. The wrong choice can spell disaster.

Liabilities

Balance Your Balance Sheet, Part II

It's no secret that many of us build our economic future on borrowed funds. That's not always a bad thing, but too much of anything can create problems. We call these obligations liabilities and, in the world of personal finance, they can play a big role in how we live our lives. These obligations come with significant costs. For example, buying a home involves one of the greatest liabilities many of us will ever assume: a mortgage. A mortgage is a sizeable obligation with the costs to match. Many of us use credit cards to finance our regular purchases and, as a result, incur hefty charges when we carry a balance. If we attend college, chances are that student loans will cover part of the tab. Of course, that comes at a price. Get the picture? Most of us will have liabilities on our personal balance sheet and, while these debts are not all bad, having too many can be a problem. The most common personal finance liabilities include the following:

- Home mortgage
- Auto loans
- Student loans
- Credit card balances
- Other

In later chapters, we will take a closer look at each of these common liabilities and what you need to know about each one. In this chapter, we will take a look at several issues:

- The pros and cons of liabilities
- Good debt vs. bad debt
- Common liabilities

- To borrow or not to borrow
- Compounding interest

The Pros and Cons of Liabilities

A fear of debt is often a fear of opportunity. Imagine if you lived your life debt free:

No mortgage = no house

No school loans = no education

No credit cards = no shopping

On the other hand, if you avoided assuming liabilities your whole life, you might enjoy a high level of economic freedom. We've all met the blowhard at the cocktail party who likes to brag about the fact that his house is paid for, his school is paid for, and he's off to Cabo for the fifth time this year. Well, let's give credit where credit is due. He worked hard (or married well) and was able to avoid taking on the debt that afflicts so many of us. His life is on cruise control and while the rest of us struggle to pay our bills, well, he seems to live in a different realm. Enough about our braggart friend. The fact is that little to no debt can offer significant flexibility and freedom. So, is it better to live debt free or to pile on the debt? That depends. Let's consider both sides of the argument.

Why Liabilities Are Good

They create opportunities. Without them, it would be difficult to improve your skills, enhance your career, or just live a better life.

They provide liquidity. In the age of credit, opportunity may exist even though cash does not. Through borrowing, you can fill in the gaps when cash falls short.

They help you achieve your goals sooner rather than later. Assuming liabilities can allow you to capitalize on an opportunity sooner rather than later. No need to wait until you earn the money to enroll in school and start a business—the funds are available through various lending institutions.

Why Liabilities Are Bad

They can be overwhelming. Take on too many liabilities and you may never pay them off. It's as simple as that.

They can hurt your credit. As we discussed earlier, too many liabilities can create cash-flow problems for you. While your income may drop, your debt service remains the same. Before long, you might find yourself working just to meet your monthly interest payment. And if you can't make the payment, your credit score may drop. This can create a downward credit death spiral making it harder for you to refinance your debts and, ultimately, create a near hopeless financial situation.

They can hurt your net worth. With each additional liability you assume, your net worth may decrease. This is not always the case, and it really depends on the reason behind the liability. For example, borrow to purchase real estate and you might fare well if the value of the real estate increases. On the other hand, borrow off of credit cards to purchase shoes and guess what? You could end up in financial purgatory.

Good Debt vs. Bad Debt

The following cases illustrate the broad differences between good debt and bad debt. Can you figure out which is which?

Case 1: Jimmy just got a credit card with a $1,000 limit. He maxed out with his first purchase of a flat-screen TV.

While this may help Jimmy's credit score, it could also cause big problems later. A flat-screen TV is nice, but it won't help Jimmy's financial situation. TVs are highly depreciable and while Jimmy can certainly enjoy his favorite reality shows, he's financing an item that will soon be worth a lot less.

Answer: Bad

Case 2: Jenny just borrowed $20,000 for her first year of college.

Student loans can be oppressive but, assuming the terms are reasonable, this debt helps pave the way to a better future. Jenny will likely parlay her education into a more fulfilling and more lucrative career. If all goes well, she'll be able to pay off the loan in a reasonable amount of time.

Answer: Good

Case 3: Tony bought a house. He put $20,000 down and got a mortgage for $80,000.

Assuming Tony can afford the monthly payments and the mortgage terms are reasonable, this may prove a wise choice. Tony has a place to live and, hopefully, that place will appreciate in value over the years. Of course, this doesn't always happen so Tony will need to make sure he's getting a fair purchase price and the mortgage terms are favorable.

Answer: Good

Case 4: Denise bought a jet ski. The store that sold it worked out a rent-to-own agreement with monthly payments of $80 per month over five years.

Answer: Bad

If you're not sure about this one, you need to reread this chapter. Highly depreciable asset plus rent-to-own equals bad idea. No way. Case closed.

Common Liabilities

The liabilities below tend to show up on most personal balance sheets. We'll cover the basics of each now and explore them in more detail in later chapters.

Home Mortgages

Chances are if you are a homeowner, you carry some type of mortgage. The mortgage can be used to finance a small amount or the vast majority of your home's purchase price. The great thing about home mortgages is that they make homeownership a reality for many people who would otherwise have difficulty saving enough to purchase an entire home with cash. With average home prices in the six-figure range, few can afford such princely sums. But, by borrowing much of that amount, a home purchase is suddenly a real possibility.

Auto Loans

Cars, like homes, are often too difficult to buy with cash. The auto loan offers an affordable way to purchase a car, which is a necessity for many people. While public transportation can be efficient and cost-effective (not to mention highly entertaining), many of us do not have access to it. Unfortunately, a car is sometimes the only way to get to and from work. Coming up with thousands of dollars for such a purchase can prove a major challenge. Fortunately, car manufacturers, car dealers, and lending institutions are all more than willing to lend you the money for the right price. Again, the key here is to make sure that price, or interest rate, is as low as it can be.

Credit Card Balances

What can one say about credit card balances that hasn't already been said? While credit cards can be a terrific way to track your expenses and earn rewards points, carrying a balance can be a nightmare. The interest rates on these balances can easily fall in the double-digit range and, before long, you just might find yourself struggling to cover the interest. Your best bet is to pay all credit card balances in full each and every month. Period.

Tony's Liabilities		
Mortgage on Miami Mansion	4	million
Credit Card Debt	0.5	million
Auto Loans	0.1	million
Other Borrowings from Various Business Associates	1	million
Total Liabilities	**5.6**	**million**

Figure 2-1. Sample liabilities section of balance sheet

Tony's success did not come without a price. Aside from participating in some less-than-ethical activities, he assumed a reasonable amount of debt as shown in Figure 2-1. Were these financial moves justified?

To Borrow or Not to Borrow

Not all liabilities are bad provided they are structured under favorable terms. So, how do you determine when to borrow? Consider the following checklist:

- Am I borrowing to purchase something I need or something that will increase in value?
- Is my cost of borrowing reasonable?
- Can I afford the monthly payments?

If you answered yes to all three of these, then perhaps it's worth considering a loan of some sort.

Compounding Interest

Here are two of the most important days of my life:

1. The day I learned that Darth Vader was really Luke's father (sorry about omitting the spoiler alert, but if you haven't seen *The Empire Strikes Back*, please stop reading this book and watch the *Star Wars* series).

2. The day I learned about compounding interest. As many will tell you, this is arguably one of the most powerful forces in the universe. (At least Einstein is rumored to have said this, so you know it's big. And if it's on the Internet, it must be true.)

Since this is a finance book, we'll focus on compounding interest. Compounding interest is interest earning interest on itself. In other words, money grows over time because interest earns interest on itself. This can be great for investors and terrible for debt holders. Take a look at the effects of compounding interest when borrowing:

Compounding Interest Example 1

Item: MP3 player

Price: $199

Interest Rate: 19.99%

Monthly Payments $10

Time to Pay Off: 24 months

Total Cost: $239![1]

Compounding Interest Example 2

Item: Vacation

Price: $2,500

Interest Rate: 19.99%

Monthly Payments $42

Time to Pay Off: 216 months

Total Cost: $9,041![2]

If you're not careful, compounding interest can prove devastating. The vacation above will end up costing you nearly four times the original price! Sadly, many of us fall victim to this. Consider the dangers of compounding interest:

1. It can grow fast.

2. You can pay several times more than what you borrowed.

3. While you are making payments, you cannot use money for other purchases you might want or need.

4. It can affect your credit score and your ability to borrow for more important things.

---

[1] Source: TheMint.org

[2] Ibid.

Chapter Lessons

- Not all debt is bad. We've seen that borrowing is a fact of life and, when done wisely, it can create opportunities.

- Be aware of all the terms associated with debt. When financing a purchase, always remember to make sure the interest rate is low and fixed, make sure you make your payments on time each month, and be aware of other fees.

- Make sure your purchase is something you can justify. Ideally, finance things that will appreciate in value or increase your earning potential. And if this is not the case, make sure it is something you absolutely need.

Equity
Balance Your Balance Sheet, Part III

The final and most often misunderstood part of the balance sheet is what we call *equity*. Equity is a common topic of discussion in the business world. From real estate to the stock market, deals revolve around it. Ultimately, everyone wants to know how much of something they own. In personal finance, equity is built around similar principles. Equity gives us an indication of how much we actually own after accounting for what we owe. Equity is the difference between assets and liabilities. If assets exceed liabilities, you are actually worth something (financially speaking, of course). And if liabilities exceed assets, well … let's just say we have some work to do.

Equity can determine what direction your life takes. Maintain a negative equity balance and chances are your opportunities will decrease while your prospects for bankruptcy increase. As I mentioned earlier in the book, your goal is to build wealth so that wealth works for you. Equity plays a major role in this. Now the fun part. On your personal balance sheet, this represents (drum roll, please), your personal net worth. It's sad, but many people measure their accomplishments in life largely based on this number. More importantly, this number is a term we often associate with celebrities. You read about private car collections, multiple homes, and rankings on the Forbes 400. While those maintaining higher numbers can afford the doggie therapist, this number has more bearing than simple lifestyle enhancement. Even those of us with far less aggressive ambitions can make use of this number. In this chapter, we will discuss these topics:

- Why is net worth so important?

- How to calculate net worth

- How to grow net worth

Why Is Net Worth So Important?

Why is this number so important? How do we calculate it? Who cares? Let's start with the last one first. You should care. And maybe that person you met at a club on South Beach might care. Basically, your net worth is just a number and what is considered adequate really depends on what your goals are in life. Without question, this number must be positive. That may not always be the case, but the goal is to make sure it is positive, and maximizing it will depend on what you intend to do with it.

Assets – Liabilities = Equity (personal net worth)

Equity = Net Worth

Net worth is the number that helps you determine your health grade. If the number is positive, breathe a sigh of relief because you're financially healthy. The bigger question, however, is just how healthy? Can you run a sprint? A marathon? Your financial health is often related to your age just as your personal health report is. The difference, however, is an inverse relationship between age and financial health. In other words, the older you get, the healthier your personal balance sheet must be.

In business finance and in personal finance, taking total assets and subtracting total liabilities will determine equity. If you buy a home for $500,000 by paying $100,000 down and borrowing $400,000, you have $100,000 of equity at the time of purchase. If the home value appreciates to $600,000 and you still have the $400,000 mortgage outstanding, your equity is now $200,000. In other words, if you have more than you owe, your net worth is positive. Seems like a simple goal to aspire to but, surprisingly, many of us are not in this position and, as such, headed for major challenges ahead. Think of negative net worth as receiving your doctor's report to find that you have just been diagnosed with a major illness. Depending on how significant this negative number is, the prognosis may not be good. Not hopeless, just not good. When it comes to personal finance, the doctor's report will never state your condition as terminal. That's the beauty of personal finance. It can, however, be pretty bad and indicate a long and painful road to recovery. Enough bad news. Let's talk about the good news. The good news is that now you know where you stand and if you read the rest of this book, you will acquire the tools to get to where you want to be.

How to Calculate Net Worth

1. Make a list of all of your assets.

2. Segment your assets into liquid and illiquid.

3. Segment your assets into income producing and non-income producing.

4. Total your assets.

5. List all of your liabilities.

6. Total your liabilities.

7. Subtract your total liabilities from your total assets.

How to Grow Net Worth

1. Limit your spending and increase your savings.

2. Purchase appreciable assets.

3. Pay down high-interest debts.

4. Convert liabilities to assets.

In Figure 3-1, we have all the pieces in place to build Tony's complete balance sheet. Given that his assets are valued at $21 million and his liabilities $5.6 million, his net worth is $15.4 million. Tony has truly achieved the American Dream. The world is his. However, one problem presents itself: Tony's assets are for the most part illiquid. Sure, it's great that he has solid investments, but few of them could be liquidated in an emergency. Aside from the cash he holds, it would be difficult to convert the other items to cash on short notice. And for an entrepreneur like Tony, that could be a problem.

Tony's Assets		
Cash	2	million
Miami Mansion	5	million
Petting Zoo	1	million
Wife's Jewelry	1	million
Cars	1	million
Boats	2	million
Furniture (including custom-made fountain)	1	million
Stock (shares in various Colombian-based commodities companies)	8	million
Total Assets	**21**	**million**

Tony's Liabilities		
Mortgage on Miami Mansion	4	million
Credit Card Debt	0.5	million
Auto Loans	0.1	million
Other Borrowings from Various Business Associates	1	million
Total Liabilities	**5.6**	**million**
Tony's Equity (Net Worth)	**15.4**	**million**

Figure 3-1. Tony's complete balance sheet

Keeping Track of Your Net Worth

When it comes to celebrities and CEOs, net worth is talked about as much as lifestyle. It's difficult to ignore these numbers, which show up as often in business journals as they do in the tabloids. Our tendency is to assume this is a number uniquely associated with those who shuttle the globe in private jets. The reality, however, is that each of us needs to calculate this number and watch it closely. We don't need to become obsessed with it. We'll leave the obsession over this number to personal wealth managers and Wall Street moguls. For our purposes, it's important to check this number periodically. Four times a year at a minimum is recommended. Keeping track of your net worth helps you plan your financial activities and adjust your lifestyle accordingly. Most of all, it will give you an indication in terms of how close you are to achieving your financial goals.

Consider the case of Ben. Ben just graduated from a prestigious East Coast college and has since moved out west to his parents' home. He spends his days lounging in their swimming pull, cruising in his Alfa Romeo convertible, and helping out the wife of his dad's business partner. Ben's personal balance sheet, and, more specifically, his net worth are not in good shape. Take a look.

His assets consist of cash, a bus pass, and an Alfa Romeo. His liabilities consist of credit card debt and student loans.

Based on Ben's balance sheet, Figure 3-2, his net worth is ($37,980). Note that the negative value is shown in parentheses. He's in the hole and a long ways from climbing out.

Assets			
	Cash	$	5,000
	Bus Pass	$	20
	Alfa Romeo	$	10,000
	Total	$	15,020
Liabilities			
	Credit Card Debt	$	3,000
	Student Loans	$	50,000
	Total	$	53,000
Equity			
(Net Worth)		$	(37,980)

Figure 3-2. Ben's net worth without a job

So, what does Ben do? Well, he gets a job in plastics. Now, with a job and a solid savings plan, he's well on his way to turning his net worth from negative to positive, as shown in Figure 3-3. Before long, he will be financially healthy and well on his way to marrying his dream girl, Elaine. Or, at least spending time with her and her mother.

Assets			
	Cash	$	80,000
	Bus Pass	$	20
	Alfa Romeo	$	10,000
	Total	$	90,020
Liabilities			
	Credit Card Debt	$	3,000
	Student Loans	$	50,000
	Total	$	53,000
Equity			
(Net Worth)		$	37,020

Figure 3-3. Ben's net worth with a job

Chapter Lessons

- Building equity is key to building financial freedom. Assets are important and liabilities are important, but our ultimate goal is to ensure that we have more assets than liabilities. That difference forms equity or what we often refer to as net worth.

- There is no ultimate net worth number. We each have our own goals in terms of what is the right net worth number, but we should all aspire to have a positive net worth number.

- Building net worth is a lifetime process. It doesn't happen overnight, and it begins with a focus on maximizing assets and minimizing liabilities.

Financial Feng Shui— Get Organized!

Sure, this is a personal finance book, but what I forgot to mention is that this book is anything but conventional. This is why I'm ducking conventional form and addressing one of the most important matters in all of personal finance: how to get your act together. Since you bought this book, you very well just might have problems organizing your finances. And if you do have superior financial organization skills and you still bought this book, all I can say is, "Great seeing you at the reunion, and I'll reimburse you soon." In order to achieve the highest level of success in personal finance, it's important to make sure you stay organized. This avoids wasting time and money. This chapter focuses on the following topics:

- Freeing your mind and your space
- Avoiding charges and late fees
- Negotiating lower rates

Freeing Your Mind and Your Space

I don't profess to be an expert in feng shui, nor do I completely understand it. I will say that some years ago, after picking up the discarded beer cans and dirty laundry from the floor of my apartment, my dating life improved dramatically. Go figure. I now espouse the basic tenants of this philosophy and, above all, believe in the virtues of staying organized. One of the greatest lessons I've learned is to maintain current and organized financial records. Here's how.

Paperless

Go paperless as much as possible. This not only eliminates physical clutter but also saves time and money. All you need is a basic scanner, which you can grab for under a hundred bucks. Some smartphone apps can actually turn your phone's camera into a scanner, which may have mixed results depending on the scanned document's level of detail. In any case, figure out which solution works for you and get started.

What should you scan? If you asked me, I'd say everything, but let's focus on the financial documents. Bills, receipts, and financial statements are a good starting point. Scanning them allows you to save them to your computer, eliminating the need for bulky drawers. More importantly, you can access any of the documents easily without having to rummage through a stack of papers. This can prove particularly handy at tax time or the next time you apply for a mortgage. While the document assembly process can take hours for most people seeking to apply for a mortgage, it can be done in a matter of minutes if you hold the documents in electronic format. Just make sure you keep your electronic files organized. I suggest creating file folders for each bill type and naming the individual files by billing date (for example, "phone_March_2013").

Hanging Folders

So, you're still one of those old-school types. Fair enough. Skip the scanner and, at the very least, invest ten bucks in a simple, portable hanging file holder. Make sure you can flip it open from the top and view separate file folders for each of your bills. You can pick this holder up and carry it over to the kitchen table and take it to your accountants or even to your future in-laws when you have to negotiate a dowry.

Avoiding Charges and Late Fees ... Like the Plague

When I was a first grader, I decided that the best way to earn the respect of my playground peers was to mouth off to the older kids. While it would be easier to bully the kindergartners, I felt that this practice would simply yield less than desirable results. So, I took the David and Goliath approach and went for the biggest, nastiest fifth grader I could find. In front of my first-grader minions, I made up a little song about his name and how bad he smelled. Clearly irked by this general lack of respect, he chased me off the playground and into the fields. I hadn't managed to formulate a plan for how to evade capture at this point as I was savoring the chorus of applause from the first-grade cheering section. As I made efforts to return back to the playground, I felt my chest tighten and my speed slow. The last time I felt this way, my mom and dad stuffed an inhaler in my mouth. Yup, I was having an asthma attack. I could barely breathe and running was nearly impossible. At that moment, what felt like a bear paw swatted me across the shoulder and knocked me to the ground. The fifth-grade bear was sitting on top of me. He smiled, cocked his fist, and punched me in the nose. My eyes filled with tears and my nostrils with blood. All of a sudden, I forgot about my asthma attack and focused on my bloody nose. I learned two good lessons that day: (1) A new problem will only hide an old problem, but the old problem won't go away; (2) Don't pick on smelly fifth graders. Let's focus on the first.

One of the best ways to make a bad financial situation even worse is to miss payment deadlines, which can trigger interest payments and penalties. Before long, you can find yourself struggling to pay these fees and will have all but forgotten about the principal. Suddenly, your new problem hides your old one while the old one is the source of the new problem. I can't tell you how many people I've met who find themselves in this situation. A friend of mine was literally devoting nearly every paycheck to paying interest and penalties on her credit card balances. This creates a downward financial cycle, which, unless some serious steps are taken, will not end well. Avoid these fees and penalties at all costs and you will thank me later. I'll settle for you naming your next kid, grandkid, or even pet after me.

Auto Pay / Automated Clearing House (ACH)

One of the greatest inventions since the printing press is ACH, or what is commonly termed "auto pay." This nifty system allows you to set up an online account with your bank and designate a list of accounts to whom payments should be made. Your monthly payment for each account will be deducted from your bank account on the date it is due. You will usually receive a monthly e-mail or text message confirming the amount that was deducted. This system all but eliminates the hassles and costs of mailing checks. It also eliminates the clutter of bills that can end up decorating your kitchen table. And, best of all, it virtually eliminates the risk of missing a payment. Of course, you have to make sure your bank account doesn't run on empty or you could be dealing with bigger problems with your bank comes calling.

Online Bill Pay

Online bill pay allows you to designate your bill recipients on your bank's web site. Spend a few minutes to set this up and it will save you countless hours, and dollars, each year. When your next bill comes in, simply log on to your bank's web site, select "bill pay," type the amount owed, and press "send." What normally took you five minutes to do plus the cost of a stamp and envelope now takes ten seconds and is free. This gives you a bit more control and flexibility than auto pay but requires you to take the time to log on to your bank's web site.

Bill Calendar

OK, so you're stuck in your ways and insist on doing things the old-fashioned way. Some people actually look forward to assembling their bills once a month and writing checks for each. I imagine these are the same people who read printed books, don't own mobile phones, and prefer a real conversation over e-mail. What's wrong with you people! If you fall into this category, so be it. At the very least, make sure you set bill reminders in a bill calendar. If you do happen to use a mobile phone or computer, it should be easy enough to set reminders on your calendar. And if you shun modern conveniences like electricity, grab one of the freebie calendars from your local realtor and list the days of the month that your bills come due. Examples include rent, mortgage payment, condo fees, utilities, phone, cable, insurance (all types), and credit card. In some cases, credit card companies and other companies may allow you to designate your billing date. If possible, try to arrange your billing statement date and due date to fall within the same time frame (within a week or so of one another) so that you can sit down and do your bills all at once.

Negotiating Lower Rates

Ever found yourself on the phone with a call center rep and on the verge of smashing your phone into a million pieces? If so, this section is for you. Whether it's the cable company, phone company, or credit card company, dealing with phone reps is only slightly less unnerving than a spinal tap. The problem is that most phone reps are trained to get you off the phone as quickly as possible without losing your account. The fact is that your account is your greatest strength in these discussions. Keep this in mind when trying to negotiate lower rates and consider the following adage: Know your strengths. How much are you paying monthly and how much have you paid since you opened your account? If you pay $100 per month for cable and have been a loyal customer for ten years, guess what? You've given the cable company $12,000 of your hard-earned money. Over the next several months, that can add up to a sizeable sum, one that the company would rather not lose which affords you a clear advantage when negotiating.

And another piece of advice: Know your options. If you drop your cable company, can you go somewhere else? If you have a large credit card balance and are paying a high rate of interest, you might consider a balance transfer to a different card. Trust me—the credit card company doesn't want to lose you. It's important to know your options and be ready to express them.

Finally, get to the right person. Don't waste your time with the first person who takes your call. Your goal should be to speak to a decision maker, preferably a manager.

Armed with these pieces of information, you're ready for battle. It's important to remind yourself that the people you speak with are doing their job and deal with angry customers all the time. If you can show them a little respect, maybe some kindness, you just might advance your cause. Ask them how their day is going. Ask for their name in case you get disconnected. Having this information will help in case the call is dropped and will give you credibility in case any follow-up is needed. Back to our story. Once you get the call rep on the line, explain that you're very disappointed because you no longer feel valued as a customer. Your monthly rate is too high, and you have other options. You believe in loyalty and would hate to close your account but, at the same time, cannot afford to pay such high rates. Stress how much you've paid in total since you've had your account open (to remind them just how valuable you are). Finally, ask them what they can do to bring your rate down and keep you as a customer. Hopefully, they start to offer you some options. If they resist, as a last resort, you can always say that you would like to be transferred to account deactivations in order to understand what next steps are needed to close your account. They may pass you on to someone more senior who helps you or to customer retention. Sometimes, they just don't care and will send you to deactivation. At that point, it's up to you how you want to proceed. If you are not committed to closing your account, ask the rep in deactivation for a list of procedures associated with deactivation and mention that you're still weighing your options. Get off the phone as there is nothing worse than an empty threat.

Call Rep: Good afternoon, Scamtron Cable. How may I help you?

Me: Hi, there. How's your day going?

Call Rep: Fine, sir. Yours?

Me: Well, not great.

Call Rep: I'm sorry to hear that. What seems to be the problem?

Me: Well, I'm just not feeling valued as a customer.

Call Rep: I'm so sorry to hear that. How might I help you?

Me: That depends. I'm sorry; I didn't catch your name.

Call Rep: It's Brittany.

Me: That's a beautiful name. I can tell my day is getting better already.

Call Rep: You're very sweet.

Me: It's been a long time since someone has said that. Brittany, would it be too forward of me to ask you to coffee sometime?

Call Rep: That would be great. Do you live in Chennai?

(OK, let's back up to the call rep saying "How might I help you?")

Me: I'd like to discuss ways to lower my monthly bill because, frankly, I have several options from your competitors who are eager for my business. I value your service and would hate to leave given that I've spent $12,000 with you since I became a customer. I just can't justify what I'm paying now, especially with so many other options out there.

Hopefully, you'll get results. If nothing else, ask for a one-time credit as a courtesy. You can always call back in few months and try for better rates. You never know. I once had a rep tell me to call direct every six months for a rate reduction. We became good buddies. I was devastated when I found out he had been fired. Who would have thought?

Chapter Lessons

- Keep your bill payment system streamlined and automated to avoid late fees.

- Go paperless whenever possible and you will save time, space, and money.

- Always negotiate lower rates.

The Personal Finance Panacea— Make More Money!

One of the most important matters in all of personal finance is how to earn more money. These matters are often addressed on infomercials, but perhaps it's worth making mention of a few points that could help you with your career and just might put a few extra bucks in your pocket. While this chapter may have a slight corporate job bias, the concepts apply to just about anyone from business manager to farmer.

In this chapter, we'll cover two topics:

- Landing your dream job
- Getting promoted

Landing Your Dream Job

One job has eluded me my entire life. It surprises me because I was able to land offers at some of Wall Street's most selective banks coming out of school. Prior to that, one major corporation repeatedly shot me down. I tried everything from follow-up phone calls, informational interviews, and even proposed a trial employment period. After submitting several applications and making dozens of phone calls, I resigned myself to the fact that I would never be a McDonald's cashier.

We all have our dream job, but landing it is something few of us prepare for. The following steps can help:

1. Target your job search. Figure out what you're good at and what you're qualified for. Once you've done this, get ready to make your move.

2. Polish your résumé. Clean up each line to convey the skills that highlight what is needed to land your targeted position.

3. Network online and in person. Social networks such as LinkedIn are great for this. They allow you to not only tap into your own personal network but other networks as well. Clearly, one of the greatest developments of the twenty-first century.

4. Schedule interviews. Whether you find specific job postings or discover companies that you would like to work for, start arranging interviews. If you're not invited, ask for an informational one. They are a great way for you to showcase yourself and learn more about the company. While this may not lead to your dream job immediately, it shows initiative and just might impress someone who will call you the next time a position opens up.

5. Follow up. Send handwritten thank-you cards to everyone you meet. If you don't hear back, don't worry. This will impress someone and, when the time comes, you will move to the top of the list.

If You Keep Jumping Ship, You Will Drown

It's important to stay focused. I have too many friends who change jobs as frequently as most of us change clothes. This lack of focus is clear to any prospective employer and can lead to a very short career. Stay focused on finding that dream job and stick with it. Most jobs are tough in the beginning, and it's up to you to give it time to work.

Getting Promoted

Whether or not you have landed your dream job, you should always strive to get ahead in any job. Follow these tips and not only will you earn more, it may help you to land a better job in the future.

Perception Is Everything

One of my favorite episodes of the TV classic *Seinfeld* is the episode in which George Costanza pretends to be under heavy pressure at work. This, of course, was a clever way to avoid responsibility and impress his superiors. Through fits of impatient sighs, he convinces nearly everyone that he's the busiest guy at the office and involved with some very important work. I can't tell you how many times I've observed this kind of behavior in the workplace and, invariably, it proves effective. Pretending to be stressed and busy will not guarantee you success. However, acting too cool and relaxed can give others the impression that you simply do not have enough to do. Here is my list of workplace behaviors to boost your work image in the eyes of your colleagues and superiors:

Keep conversations short. Watercooler banter can be a colossal waste of time, so if you're eager to offer your insights on who should have won the big game, save it. You've got more important things cooking and your colleagues need to see that.

One drink maximum at work events. During my frat-boy days, nursing a beer all night would earn me a session of systematic hazing at the next chapter meeting. In the professional world, it pays to stay sober, so leave the drinking for nights out with your friends. Business is about business whether it's during the day or at night. Sure, the peer pressure is relentless, but I've seen far too many careers torpedoed by that fourth martini. No one I know ever lost a promotion for not drinking enough.

Keep your desk organized but not empty. Stacks of files and papers are fine as long as you can find what you're looking for and people know you're busy. An empty desk indicates you have too much free time, and one resembling the city dump indicates you just might be one step away from a Jerry Maguire office meltdown.

Send e-mails early morning and late night. The boss will love this, and your underlings will know you mean business. It shows that work is a priority for you no matter how early or how late in the day.

First in, last out. Your bosses won't remember the great animation you selected for your PowerPoint presentation, but they will remember if you are the first one at the office in the morning and the last one to leave the office at night.

Meeting Management

Here is where you can really shine. How you manage a meeting and what you say during it defines you. Remember to speak first and, if possible, speak last. Speaking first helps set the tone, exhibits your leadership qualities, and allows you to steer the meeting. Speaking last gives your boss and coworkers something to remember you by especially if you take charge and summarize the meeting points as well as the next steps to be taken. Suddenly, you're respected by your peers as the de facto boss, and your own boss respects you as a qualified deputy.

Public Speaking

Jump on this. I know it's terrifying, but my advice is for you to do everything possible to get over your fear of public speaking and volunteer to speak at every event. Panel discussions, roundtable discussions, industry trade shows— do whatever it takes. Become a thought leader and remember that it's not so much what you say but that you're willing to say it. The fact that you have the guts to stand up and speak in front of a large group sets you apart from everyone else who clings to the sidelines.

Become a Profit Center, Not a Cost Center

One of the best lessons I took away from my days in a corporate cubicle was that there are two types of people in the world: cost-center people and profit-center people. Both types are vital to the success of any organization, and you can't have one without the other. However, one gets most of the respect and the other very little. Can you guess which one gets all the respect? In most companies, you'll find people in sales and marketing from entry level to senior management. Each is responsible for driving business growth, and their success is measured in terms of how much they contribute to the company's sales initiatives. These people are profit-center people. On the other hand, you have the legal, finance, accounting, and human resource people. They make sure the business runs smoothly. These are the cost-center people. Now, most of us rational people recognize the need for both profit- and cost-center people but, in times of crisis, corporate managers don't always see things so clearly. Unfortunately, the cost-center people are usually the first to get the pink slips while the profit-center folks are often rewarded. When AIG teetered on the verge of collapse, layoffs became a daily occurrence. And while the cost-center people headed for cover, the profit-center people were praised and rewarded. In fact, AIG announced a Vegas boondoggle for their top salespeople! Say what you will about this move, but the lesson here is simple: The business world rewards the profit-center folks and often ignores the cost-center folks. Spoiler alert: The boondoggle was canceled.

So, what does this have to do with personal finance? Well, if you're a cost-center person, more power to you. Frankly, most of my friends are cost-center folks and, as a business manager, I often find myself focused on cost-center activities more than profit-center activities. The lesson for us, however, is to manage our personal financial dealings from the perspective of a cost center and our careers from the standpoint of a profit center. After all, this book is ultimately about financial freedom so positioning yourself to earn more is a key contributor to this goal. Even if you are sitting in a cubicle and the boss calls you by a different name each time she sees you, all hope is not lost. Here are the steps you need to take to become a profit center whether you work in sales or office supply audit:

Demonstrate value. Whether you're counting paper clips or hiring executives, it's important that you quantify your value to your superiors. Periodic reports should detail how much you saved your company and how much value you created.

Cross-pollinate. Initiate projects with other departments to show just how much the work you do contributes to the company's bottom line.

Refer business. Even if you're internal and focused on day-to-day operations, it doesn't mean you can't sell or market. Opportunities present themselves every day, and referring business to the right people can never hurt.

Network. Get to know everyone. The more people you know (assuming you're not a jerk), the more opportunities you create for yourself.

Be visible. Any chance to put your name on something, take it. As mentioned before, public speaking opportunities are even better. Best of all, if you can demonstrate expertise in any one area, go for it. You could soon find yourself ordained a thought leader. Being the best at purchasing office chairs is better than being a mediocre sales rep. Be the best and make sure everyone knows it. It's OK to be an unsung hero in your personal life, but work is a different story.

Control your expenses. Managing your workplace expenses is just as important as your personal ones. You are part of an organization and someone is signing your expense reports. I have seen countless people hurt their chances for promotion by maxing out their expense accounts. Always spend a little less than you are allowed to and someone will notice.

Never stop learning. Sign up for continuing education classes, lunchtime seminars, and anything else that will allow you to enhance your skills. Not only will you benefit from it personally, but your peers and superiors will recognize your passion for expanding your knowledge base. There is no better way to show that you are grooming yourself for a leadership role than to take this approach and be as visible as possible about it. In the end, the more you learn about your company, the farther you will go within it.

Chapter Lessons

- Managing your career effectively and excelling at what you do is one of the best things you can do for your finances.

- Land your dream job and you will be motivated to do your best. There is always room for advancement and presenting yourself as someone who is smart, poised, and professionally curious will help you get ahead ... which means a fatter bank account.

- Perception and passion rule the day. Your peers and your superiors should see you as someone who puts work above everything.

Budgeting and Saving— Oh, No!

Look, tonight is the future, and I am planning for it. There's this shirt I gotta buy, a beautiful shirt.

—Tony Manero, *Saturday Night Fever*

Back in my days as an investment banking analyst, I would carefully observe the behavior of my higher-ups. It was an enjoyable distraction and a terrific way to break up the workday. One managing director proved particularly intriguing. While he structured multimillion dollar deals and probably earned several million dollars a year in salary and bonus, he was always strapped for cash. Whether it was the seemingly endless chain of renovation expenses on his Greenwich mansion, his wife's shopping trips to Europe, or his custom-tailored suits, there was always a bill he couldn't afford to pay. I once watched him stiff the guy who shined his shoes out of a two-dollar tip! How could someone who made more money in a year than most people make in a lifetime constantly lament his financial problems? Simple. He spent more than he earned. In the world of finance, if you spend more than you earn, you'll find yourself in big trouble. OK, you can put the book down because you've learned the most important lesson I have to offer. Common sense, right? Yet individuals, corporations, and even governments fail to observe this basic rule.

The only way to consistently and effectively observe this rule is to create a budget.

Calculating a budget is one of the most difficult tasks many of us will ever face, at least in personal finance. Few of us like budgeting as it causes us to self-impose rules. Thinking about the budget can often take the fun out of many of life's simple pleasures. Do you really want to order a Pabst Blue Ribbon when you're craving a Stoli martini? Do you want to sleep at Howard Johnson's or the Ritz? We can all appreciate the finer things in life, and there's no shame in wanting them. However, if chasing them causes you to compromise your financial future, perhaps it's time to reprioritize and budget.

Let's consider why we budget. Corporations do this on a regular basis. Individuals, departments, and the entire company will destroy millions of trees and consume billions of computer bytes in the process of budgeting. How much will you spend on ballpoint pens this quarter? Three-ring binders? Pizza parties? Accounting? Legal fees? Marketing? Did you spend too much? Too little? It's enough to drive even the most adroit business manager crazy. Nonetheless, a company cannot thrive without a budget. It lends perspective to the direction and growth of a business. If a company fails to budget, it runs the risk of spending more than it earns and that can pave the way to Chapter 11 bankruptcy. So why don't we take this approach in our personal lives? I've met dozens of corporate executives who can drive their own departments to sky-high profitability but, when it comes to their own personal finances, they're a few days away from a visit from the repo man.

It's not all bad. Putting together a budget for the purpose of boosting your savings can be fun. After all, keeping more of what you work so hard for can be a good thing. If you're saving more, you're getting closer to the point of financial Nirvana when your money works for you. So, let's get started.

In this chapter, we look at these topics:

- Steps to building a budget
- Maximizing your budget (without ruining your life)
- Saving for a sunny day
- Reasons to save
- Seizing opportunity through saving
- What saving can do for you
- Being a smart saver

Steps to Building a Budget

While the entire process can be daunting and sometimes complex, breaking things down to a few simple steps can help:

1. First, make a list of all of your possible monthly and annual expenses. Annual expenses will need to be divided by 12 to keep things consistent on a monthly basis.

2. Next, calculate your estimated after-tax income. Your final year-end number may vary, but your monthly take-home income should give you a good rough idea.

3. Total both columns and calculate the difference. If the difference is positive, you're on the right track. Negative, well, that's why you bought the book, right? Now the fun starts. Making improvements to your budget is just as important as building one in the first place. A budget is something that must be revised on a regular basis. Once a year at a minimum and, ideally, every three months. It's important to go down the list of budget items and determine what can be reduced and what can be cut out entirely. I can help with the first part, but not the second as I'm by no means the best example of slashing indulgences. I enjoy my 700 channels of TV and premium hair-band concert tickets.

What Should Be Included

Simple—everything you spend money on. The list below should get you started, but feel free to customize it. In the end, you need a complete list of every recurring expense to compare against your after-tax income.

Living

Mortgage payment. Include principal, interest, taxes, and insurance assuming it's bundled into one monthly payment.

Rent. If you rent your home, include your monthly payment.

Heating. Whether you rent or own, what you pay on average per month should be included. This can be seasonal as most people pay more in the winter than summer, so take a look at your total spending from last year and calculate a monthly average.

Water and sewer. Again, one of those things we often ignore, but it's a cost nonetheless. Take stock and calculate your monthly payment.

Electricity. Same as heating.

Telephone (landline) and Internet. Check your monthly bill. If it varies, take a monthly average based on what you spent last year.

Telephone (mobile). Ditto. Check your monthly bill. If it varies, take a monthly average based on what you spent last year.

Cable. Check your monthly bill and make sure you include all of your cable and associated expenses including bundle packages (phone and Internet) as well as taxes and fees. Order kung-fu movies on demand once a week? Make sure you include the expense.

Grocery. What are you spending each month?

Eating out. Same as above.

Personal care (haircuts, pedicures, facials, and so on). Whether you use a FloBee or frequent a celebrity-packed boutique, make sure you list it.

Recreation, entertainment. Sports, movies, opera, mud wrestling—include it.

Medical/dental. Out-of-pocket expenses? Include.

Automobile gas and repairs. How much do you spend on gas, tune-ups, bumper stickers, spinning rims? Include the monthly total.

Public transportation. Bus, train, subway to work? Calculate your monthly payment.

Clothing. This can be nothing or a small fortune. Don't be shy. List it.

Borrowing

Credit card payments. If you carry a balance on your credit, list the monthly payment you're required to make.

Home equity loans. Have you borrowed against your home in any form besides a mortgage? List your monthly payments.

Car loans. List your monthly payment.

Car lease payments. List your monthly payment.

Insurance

Life. This will generally be an annual payment so divide it by 12.

Auto. List your monthly amount. Again, if you pay once or twice a year, make sure you calculate the monthly amount.

Home. Renter's or homeowner's insurance payments should be included here.

Health. This is a big one. Do not forget this. If you don't have health insurance, stop reading and go get it.

Investing

Savings/investments. Do you contribute to a savings or investment plan? Make sure you include the amount here.

Vacation fund. How much do you spend annually on your ice-fishing trip to Bemidji, Minnesota? Armadillo-hunting safaris in Texas? Include the cost (calculate the monthly amount) here.

Emergency fund. Are you a contingency planner? If so, congratulations. Include anything you save for the rainy-day occurrences.

Additional retirement. Do you contribute to an IRA, 401K, or any other type of retirement plan? Include the monthly contribution here.

College fund. How much do you put away for Junior's school? Four years of classes, books, housing, and beer pong can cost a fortune. If you're disciplined enough to save, include the monthly amount.

Other

Charity. Some of you actually care about helping others on a regular basis irrespective of your financial situation. If you fall into this category, I have tons of respect for you. However, you're not getting off so easy. Make sure you list your monthly contribution.

Special expenses (tuition, alimony, child support, and so forth). Supporting anyone? The groupie you met one night after a show in Cleveland? Include those payments.

Total Expenditures

Once you've calculated your total monthly expenditures, go ahead and calculate your grand total. Your next step is to take your estimated after-tax income and subtract the total expenditures. Is the number positive? If so, you're on the right track. Negative. You have some work to do. In any case, there is always room for improvement. In the next section, we'll take a look at ways to shift this budget so it's maximized.

Maximizing Your Budget

Living

Mortgage payment. In Chapter 10, I discuss ways to reduce your mortgage interest as well as monthly payment. Consider all options and select the one that accomplishes both. Having lower monthly payments but higher interest may increase your monthly cash flow, but in the long run will increase the total amount you pay. Look at refinancing your mortgage in such a way that closing costs will be minimal, your interest rate will be less, and your monthly payment will be less. This could save you a nice sum.

Rent. It's tough to renegotiate your rent if you've signed a lease, but if your lease is up for renewal, talk to your landlord about keeping it the same. Annual rent increases are common, but if you are a good tenant, your landlord just might make an exception. More importantly, losing you could mean a month or more of vacant space, which no landlord likes to endure. Feel free to stress these two points and you just might find that your landlord cuts you some slack. If you decide to move and have located your dream apartment, ask your landlord for a two-year lease instead of a one-year lease. Signing up for a longer lease just might allow you to negotiate lower monthly rent. It can't hurt to try, and landlords thrive on negotiations.

Heating. All you can do here is keep your usage down. Get in the habit of turning the heat off when you're not at home (use a timer if possible) and consider keeping your thermostat a little cooler in the winter to keep costs down. I have mixed feelings on this since I grew up in Minnesota, where most of the year is winter and heating costs can be sky high. My mom, being the household CFO, decided to keep our thermostat at a balmy 64 degrees. While I'm sure the savings were impressive, the constant chill we endured was a high price to pay. My suggestion is this: Don't go overboard unless your body can take it. More importantly, come up with creative ways to keep your home warm. Nearly every home improvement store offers tips on how to minimize energy consumption in the winter including weather stripping and insulation. And, if nothing else, invest in some nice wool sweaters.

Water and sewer. Not much you can do here unless you stop flushing the toilet, which I don't recommend.

Electricity. Don't leave lights on, don't leave the TV on, and don't run the AC nonstop. That's the best you can do. Since energy is now deregulated in many states, it pays to shop around for the lowest-cost provider.

Telephone (landline) and Internet. Unless you run a business from home, I strongly recommend getting rid of your landline. Since nearly all of us use mobile phones, there is really no need to have a landline. If reception is spotty, consider a VOIP phone, which uses your Internet connection and shouldn't cost more than a few dollars per month. You most likely need your Internet connection, but make sure you've shopped around for the lowest-cost option.

Telephone (mobile). I could write an entire book about this, but I'll spare you the gory details. I have friends who pay $50 per month and friends who pay $500 per month. I encourage most people to go for unlimited usage. It's worth paying a bit more for the peace of mind that comes with not incurring hefty overage charges. Just make sure you're getting the best rate possible. Everything is open to negotiation, so don't hesitate to call your provider and attempt to negotiate a lower rate.

Cable. I'm a confessed TV junkie so it's hard for me to give this up. At the same time, online streaming of popular shows and movies can save you a small fortune. Take a look at what you watch regularly and, if you can get it for less online, you just might consider scaling back. Most of all, make sure you negotiate the lowest rate possible with your cable company.

Grocery. I'm not going to tell you what to eat, but I will say this: Whatever you're spending could easily be less. Consider the following tips. Buy private label. Most of the time, private label or store brands are made with the same ingredients as the branded label. The big difference is that you're not paying for the marketing costs associated with the branded label. There are exceptions. I once bought store-brand ketchup that tasted like V8 mixed with saccharine. Lesson learned. I suggest trying private-label products first. If you're not thrilled, go back to the branded product. Buy in bulk. You can pay significantly less per unit, but just make sure you're not buying so much that items go to waste. Don't overstock—I've seen pantries with canned goods dating back to the Nixon era. Is this really necessary? Buy want you know you will use.

Eating out. Not much I can say here that you don't already know. Eating out can be pricey and, if you do it often, it can take a significant bite (sorry) out of your monthly budget. I like to eat out and sometimes it's simply a matter of necessity when I'm jammed with work. I have, however, learned how to indulge in these gourmet adventures without breaking my bank account. First, I rarely have more than one drink during dinner. Indeed, it's nice to down a few glasses with dinner, but I've found one glass of fine wine proves far more memorable than several of the restaurant's preferred box wine. And most of all, it tends to be far more cost-effective. Anyway, I'll leave this one up to you, but just remember that in most restaurants, two drinks can cost the same as an entrée.

Personal care (haircuts, pedicures, facials, and so on). It pays to look good so I won't tell you cut back on this. Just be smart. If your preferred hairstyle is shaved, probably no need to spend a fortune here. If you can find a barber or stylist who is just starting out, you might save a few bucks as well. Again, a very personal thing but what you save here can go a long way.

Recreation, entertainment. Nowadays, going to the movies can cost a small fortune when you factor in ticket prices, popcorn, and drinks. It's not uncommon for two people to spend $50 on a trip to the movies. Well worth it if you've waited months for that fifteenth Harry Potter sequel. But if you just like the feel of watching something on the big screen, consider this: Spend a few hundred dollars and buy an LCD project to plug into your computer. Your wall becomes your screen and, after watching ten movies, it will have paid for itself. I kid you not. The LCD projector is one of the greatest inventions ever.

Medical/dental. If you're paying too much out-of-pocket, consider upgrading your insurance.

Automobile gas and repairs. If you can minimize your use of the car, you can save a lot. Consider car-share services or carpooling. The environment will thank you.

Public transportation. Bus, trains, and subways are the way to go. And you won't find a better place to people watch.

Clothing. I could tell you to shop at thrift stores, wear hand-me-downs, or just wear the same outfit and wash it every day. Clothing is a matter of personal expression and one that is tough to compromise on. But if clothes shopping make you the best-dressed person in the poorhouse, it's time to reevaluate.

Borrowing, insurance, investing. All of these items deserve your attention, but the fact is that if you've made it this far into the book, you're already doing all you can to manage these areas. These are really not areas you can cut back on, but make sure you're not overextended in any of these areas. Your debt payments should be refinanced or renegotiated to their lowest levels, your insurance should fit your needs, your investment plan should be producing solid returns, and everything else should be justified. Enough said.

There you have it. Money-saving tips that will allow you to ultimately save more. Let's take a closer look at why saving is so important.

Saving for a Sunny Day

I met a guy in college who always smelled like detergent. I realize that some people have a penchant for clean clothes, but this guy was over the top. I can't say I minded it because detergent smells a lot better than the standard college funk emitted by college students who opt for the twice-a-week shower plan. Nonetheless, I found it rather odd that he had the time to constantly wash his clothes. Some months later, a mutual friend informed me that laundry guy was not in fact laundry guy but rather shower guy! He took three showers a day … with his clothes on. This allowed him and his clothes to stay clean while he saved a buck fifty per laundry load. This guy was a true innovator and clearly someone who saved a ton of money through this habit.

What would a personal finance book be without a section on saving? Of course, you can ignore the concept of proactively saving and hope that somehow you'll land a ten-picture deal, a contract with your favorite sports team, or inherit everything from your secret billionaire uncle. At that point, who cares about saving? There will be enough to last a lifetime no matter how much you spend. If this is not the case, however, perhaps it's time to start saving. It's important to think about saving not only for your retirement but also for opportunities that will present themselves throughout your lifetime.

Reasons to Save

If you're not sure why, then make sure you memorize this section. The basic premise here is that saving allows us to protect ourselves when our earnings diminish. More importantly, saving allows us to capitalize on opportunities. If you lose your job, you will thank your lucky stars (and your sound judgment) that you managed to save enough to live for quite some time. Obviously, it would be terrific to have enough saved to live for the rest of your life, and many of us will hopefully reach that goal. But what about those of you who are only a few years out of school or struggling to support a spouse and children? That goal may seem a ways off. It's never too soon to start. At a minimum, you should aspire to save enough to live while you find your next gig. Nowadays, that can be months if not years. The last thing you need to stress about is the all-too-common game of beat-the-clock when you're job hunting. I've seen too many careers sidetracked when people take the first job they find due to diminishing cash reserves. For example, an aspiring investment banker may find herself in a data-entry job because she doesn't have enough rent money. Once you get off your career track, it can be very difficult to get back on. So, next time you consider how much you need to save, estimate how long it could take you to find your next job and work on saving enough to cover your expenses in the event that you should find yourself in this unfortunate position.

Seizing Opportunity through Saving

Saving can also create opportunities. After my first few years in finance jobs in New York City, the 80-hour workweek grew tiresome. I decided to take some time to check out and go off the grid. I bought a one-way ticket to Costa Rica and spent the next two years of my life teaching English consulting to small businesses, and scuba diving. Not a bad setup and arguably the best two years of my life. This was all possible thanks to a determined plan to save enough to live comfortably for two years overseas. My plan consisted of strategic saving initiatives. By bringing my lunch to work, taking the train to work, and avoiding coffee breaks, I was able to save the following:

- Lunch savings—$12 per day
- Transportation savings—$10 per day
- Coffee savings—$5 per day

Total savings were $27 per day, $135 per week, $540 per month, $6,480 per year. More importantly, the amount represented $10,000 of pre-tax income all from cutting out some simple, arguably inconsequential, pleasures. The bigger issue, of course, was the reputational damage caused by these austerity initiatives. Let's just say that a single guy who carries his lunchbox and coffee thermos on the NYC subway is not necessarily going to meet America's next top model.

What Saving Can Do for You

Help you better yourself. Education is something worth investing in and, in order to do that and sleep well at night, it helps to save for it. Education can be formal, such as going to college, or informal, such as backpacking through Tibet. Either way, you're going to learn something, and the last thing you want to do when you're ready for an opportunity like this is to miss out because you can't pay for it.

Help you survive an emergency. Lose your job? Break your leg? Having money in the bank will help you manage life's adversities. Don't save and you could find yourself on crutches behind the counter at McDonalds. Remember this image the next time you decide to blow your paycheck.

Help you enjoy life. Now and in the future, this will always be the case. Having money in the bank will not only give you peace of mind, but it will help you enjoy that dream vacation, pay for your kid's wedding, or build your dream home. Nothing saved? Well, one can always dream.

Being a Smart Saver

I recently read an article on saving and one of the highlighted suggestions was to make your own laundry detergent. I kid you not. The article listed five ingredients needed to make your own laundry detergent and, if you spent the extra hour locating the Borax, washing soda, and Fels Naptha and another hour mixing the solution, you would save roughly two dollars per 24 loads! That's about eight cents per load and, if you do laundry once a week, just under five dollars per year. Woo-hoo! OK, to be fair, it might be fun to mix your own laundry detergent. It might also be fun to make your own dental floss spool out of discarded thread or make your own pencils out of charcoal. You know what else is fun? Not wasting time on mindless pursuits to save a few pennies. There are limits to frugality, and I've seen too many people miss out on some of the best things in life pursuing this type of thing. If you enjoy these things and treat them as hobbies, great. But if your only goal here is to save money, forget it. There are better, more efficient ways. Are you paying attention, extreme couponers? Being a smart saver means knowing how to save efficiently so that you derive the maximum benefit with minimal effort. Consolidating your debts with a few hours of paperwork could save you hundreds of dollars each month, but mixing your own laundry detergent probably won't. In fact, turning your home into a chemistry lab just might cause a science project-like volcano eruption. At that point, you won't only be making your own laundry detergent but your own household cleaner as well.

Chapter Lessons

- Creating a budget is a necessary step in creating a savings plan.

- Once a budget is created, maximizing it is a matter of cutting costs creatively in each line item.

- Saving money is not only important for building security but for having the ability to seize opportunities when they present themselves.

- Learn to be a smart saver and you will be able to capture opportunities without compromising your quality of life.

Shopping— Oh, Yes!

Most of us do it and, while we're not always proud of it, it is a fact of life. Unless we renounce our worldly possessions and assume the life of an ascetic, we're bound to consumerism. There's no escaping it. Here's something you won't read in most personal finance books: You should shop if it makes you happy. But there is a difference between smart shopping and dumb shopping. To better understand the art of shopping, this chapter will cover three issues:

- Dumb shopping

- Smart shopping

- Becoming a smart shopper

Dumb Shopping

Dumb shopping occurs when the idea of purchasing something conjures up the rapid flutter of a butterfly in your stomach and visions of sugarplum fairies in your head. A trip to the store to buy drain cleaner or coffee filters is pure bliss. One thing leads to another and, before you know it, you're buying Ginsu knives and pet rocks. The madness continues and you throw down the credit card for a timeshare in the Everglades. Before long, you've spent all your cash and maxed out your credit cards. Insane? Perhaps. Uncommon? No. Plenty of us will buy for the sake of buying.

Impulse buying is known to release endorphins and, while it makes us feel good, the financial damage can be lasting. It never ceases to amaze me how many of us fall prey to temptation. The allure of the wrapper, the gentle beckoning of a friendly store clerk. No one is immune. And as I sit here and write this chapter with a tinge of holier-than-thou attitude, I can't help but come clean about my own predilection for designer ties. When I started my career in investment banking, a good portion of my paycheck was blown at Barney's and Saks. Before long, I had amassed a collection of ties so large that I was stuffing them into shoe boxes for storage. My colleagues were so amused by this that they nicknamed me Giorgio Advani (sorry, it was the 90s). When I look back at what I bought and why, it smacks of dumb shopping.

So, dumb shopping is what happens when you buy something only because of the way it makes you feel at the moment. In other words, if that purchase fills you with good feelings for a short period of time, then perhaps you need to reconsider. To be honest, I can't remember more than one or two of those ties I purchased, but for me it was a quick fix, a fast way to feel good about something when most of my life revolved around working long hours. Today, I realize that buying something because it makes you feel good is not always bad. But, if you buy things regularly because they make you feel good in the moment, that can prove to be a costly and destructive habit. How destructive? Let's look at what two years of my tie purchases amounted to from a financial standpoint:

- Average price per tie: $100

- Average ties purchased per week: 2

- Number of weeks purchasing ties: 104

- Total spent on ties: $100 x 2 x 104 = $20,800!

My estimates might be a bit high because some were on sale and some were gifts, but I easily spent thousands of dollars on ties! And now I'm telling you how to manage your finances. This is riddled with irony. And it gets better. Investing $20,800 in 1996 at an annual compounded rate of interest of five percent would be worth more than double that amount today! Did I derive thousands of dollars in value from these purchases? Absolutely not. It didn't help my career, it didn't give me lasting pleasure, and it didn't even provide me with wonderful, lifelong memories. What it gave me was several storage boxes of tacky couture that I refuse to part with hoping that one day the ties will come back in style.

This experience taught me an important lesson: Shopping can be dangerous when not done correctly. To determine if your shopping habits are not only dumb but perhaps even fall in the danger zone, answer the following questions:

- Does it cause you to assume debt?

- Does your purchase make you happy for a short time?
- Five years from now, if someone gave you the money you're about to spend in exchange for the item, would you accept it?

If you answered yes to any of these questions, there's room to improve. Let's take a look at the right way to shop.

Smart Shopping

Seems a bit oxymoronic to refer to this as smart shopping, but if we're going to do it, we might as well be smart about it. In fact, shopping might even play a bigger role in wealth generation than personal income. After all, you can control your spending habits, but you can't always control your income. So here is the skinny on shopping: Do it. Depriving yourself of something you enjoy will only fuel your drive to do it and probably push you to extremes. If you learn to embrace this pursuit and accept its importance in your life, you can take control of it. In other words, don't get consumed by consumerism. Just make sure you do it the smart way.

Determine What Is Important

What do you like to buy? Are you into tchotchkes and figurines? Coffee-table books? Anything sold through an infomercial? Or do you just like to spend money. If you fall into the last category, you might need professional help. Put this book down and call your therapist. If you can't afford a therapist because you spent all your money on tchotchkes, keep reading.

The pleasure we derive from material pursuits is tough to ignore. There is a reason why we enjoy receiving gifts. Truth is, the jury is still out on whether it's better to give than receive. New items represent change and opportunities for growth. It's just plain fun to open a package with wonder while pondering how something will change your life. But like all good things, moderation is key.

Being a smart shopper means understanding what you want vs. what you need. Your needs are everything involved in maintaining your day-to-day quality of life. This varies from person to person. If you drive a Ferrari, having your car detailed becomes a need. If you drive a used Gremlin, detailing it seems a bit frivolous. Give some thought to what this means and make a list of your needs and wants.

Needs

When it comes to what you truly need, several are standouts. Without these, your quality of life will suffer:

- Household items
- Grooming supplies
- Food
- Drink
- Healthcare
- Home
- Insurance
- Transportation

Wants

Wants can sure make you happy, but you will unlikely suffer without them:

- Collectibles, art
- Expensive car
- Nice watch
- Expensive vacation
- Vacation home
- Boat

My needs list is pretty straightforward and probably not unique. How about my wants list? Not entirely unique, but here is where it gets interesting. The rule for your wants is simple: If you can afford it without borrowing and what you spend on it does not hurt your plan for retirement or your emergency fund, then it might make sense. My simple rule is this: No want should ever cost more than ten percent of your liquid net worth. Case closed. Now, there can be exceptions. Some wants can become needs and here is how. If a want can create some financial gain, it moves into the third category: Needed Wants.

Needed Wants

Above, nearly half my wants were based on rest and relaxation. Vacation, boat, vacation home. Of these three, a vacation home could end up in the needed-wants category because it is an appreciable asset. Buying it not only fulfills my personal utility objective of shirking responsibility and wasting time, but it just might make me some money. Keep in mind something like this requires a significant capital outlay and could easily violate my ten-percent rule, but it provides me with a formidable goal to turn a want into a need.

Becoming a Smart Shopper

One of my favorite TV shows growing up was *Miami Vice*. While I was too young to appreciate its sophisticated dialogue and style (I did start wearing blazers with T-shirts, however), I watched the show for one reason: Sonny Crockett's Ferrari. This little black convertible would zip through the streets and highways of South Florida with "In the Air Tonight" by Phil Collins blaring in the background. I savored these montages until one day, my world came crashing down. I learned that Crockett's car was not actually a Ferrari but a kit car assembled on a Chevy chassi! There is a lesson in all this: The smart folks at NBC saved a ton of money driving the heck out of that Chevy and people like me tuned in week after week. I'm not telling you to buy fake Rolexes and drive a fake Ferrari. Brand theft is cheesy and, in most places, illegal. What I'm saying is if you need to look good and you have to stick to a budget, no problem!

When it comes to your wardrobe, the most important secret is this: Find a good tailor. A good tailor can turn something from the $10 rack to the $100 rack. I've come a long way from thinking a suit is just a suit to making sure I have a few top-notch ones in my wardrobe. A good business outfit is an investment and one that everyone must make. I'm haunted by the line from Caddyshack: "Nice suit, really. But it looks good on you. Did you get a bowl of soup with that suit?" Time and again I've interviewed job applicants and have wanted to ask that question. You have to dress the part, and a bad look indicates amateur hour. If you're interviewing for a job, there's a good chance you don't currently have one, which means your cash flow reflects that. How do you afford nice clothes when you don't have a job? The answer is simple: tailor. Find something you can afford. Discount retailers and outlets are terrific. Buy a nice outfit, good shoes to go with it, and find the best tailor in town. He will rebuild it so that you look like you walked off the runways in Milan. Ladies, same goes for you. Buy what you can afford and make sure your accessories are sharp and tasteful. And if you must have that amazing pair of shoes with the painted sole, well, just make sure you can pay cash for it.

What to Buy on Discount

One of the best lessons from my MBA program was that many private-label products are manufactured by the same people who make the branded products. A long time ago, big-name consumer-products manufacturers figured out that they could make as much money selling things without their recognized label as they can selling similar products with their label. The difference is that the consumer pays a fraction of the price for the item without the brand name. They manufacture it, and the store that sells it slaps its own label on it and the price sensitive shopper grabs it for a fraction of the price. And, sometimes, the ingredients are identical. Beauty products, produce, household cleaners, medications—in just about every aisle in the store, you will find branded items next to private-label ones. Which ones should you buy? That is entirely up to you. I will say you can try the private-label item and, if you don't like it, go back to the brand name next time. I bought the store-brand ketchup once and learned my lesson. On the other hand, I've saved a fortune buying private-label floor cleaners. It's a small price to pay for what could amount to substantial savings over a lifetime of purchases.

Shopping can be tricky and, if you do too much of it and for the wrong reasons, it can be downright dangerous. Develop a set of principles and a system to make yourself a smart shopper.

What to Buy Online

What should you buy online? In theory, just about anything that comes from a credible source.

Books. It's difficult to screw this up and, nowadays, this is the way to go. You can sample what you're buying and download it or have it sent to you. Probably the greatest thing to happen to the book since the printing press.

Movies. Again, you can download, stream online, or have the DVD sent to you.

Music. See above.

Clothes. Only if you know your size.

Groceries. This can save you time and money. Sure, most online grocery services will charge a delivery fee, but this can be offset by finding the best bargains on the grocer's web site. These are bargains that you might otherwise miss in the store, so assuming you buy your groceries no more frequently than once a month and you buy in bulk, this could provide you with some solid cost savings.

What Not to Buy Online

Small animals. You really don't need a hamster spending three days in a UPS box.

Weapons. Do you have to ask?

Narcotics. Online or in person, I advise against this.

Big-Ticket Items

When I was a kid, we learned about this amazing invention called the VCR. I begged my dad to buy one, and he and I agreed that we needed one so that we could watch movies in our family room. He proceeded to research the VCR market, read every Consumer Reports article on the subject, and finally concluded that he needed to buy the best model available, purchase it from a world-renowned electronics distributor in New York City, and have it shipped to our home in the Midwest. He bought the item with every imaginable feature under the premise that he should spare no expense on such a sizeable purchase. The VCR arrived in the mail six weeks later, and I couldn't wait to set it up. It took my dad and me a full week to figure out how to wire it and another week to figure out how to use it. In the end, we spent more time reading the instruction manual than we did watching movies. And all of this for the low price of $1,000 ... in 1983! Moral to this story: If you don't understand the feature, don't buy it. We had tracking systems, multiple heads, self-cleaning, cruise control, anti-lock breaking, defrost ... OK, I'm exaggerating a bit, but I honestly couldn't tell you what most of the features were, and we blindly accepted them and paid for them. Even the wireless remote proved to be a pain in the neck because it never seemed to work. Lesson learned. Since then, if I buy anything, I buy it with features I understand and know I will use. This holds true for electronics, cars, and just about any other big-ticket, highly depreciable asset.

Computers

Computers are as vital as food, water, and air these days. Unfortunately, they can cost more than all three of these items combined. Nowadays, a computer should be treated as a consumable item rather than an asset purchase given the fact that its depreciation is significant. Given that you will need to buy a computer and the price tag can be hefty, I strongly encourage you to buy one with only the features you need. All too often, we end up going for the one with the bells and whistles that we never use. Features like memory and speed should be considered based on what you need now as what you think you will need in the future, but don't go overboard here. The beauty of computers is that by the time you realize you need more memory or speed, you might as well buy a new computer. Here's a way to get more life out of your computer: Every year or so, back up your files and reinstall the operating system. It's basically a reset and, in most cases, should return your computer's performance to like-new status. I've been doing this for years and have managed to save a bundle.

Small-Ticket Items

If you ever find yourself bored, grab a basket of items at your local dollar store, head to the counter, and ask, "How much is this?" At first, the response will be a polite, "One dollar." Ask again and you're likely to get "Everything is a dollar." Now, ask if you buy one item in a two pack will the price be 50 cents. This is great fun although it's likely to get you thrown out.

If you happen to watch the economic news, you know that a currency war between the U.S. and China has been going on for some time. In simple terms, China's currency is artificially low relative to the U.S. dollar and therefore Chinese goods are attractive to American consumers. What this means is that as American consumers, we can all benefit when purchasing low-cost items made in China. Enter the dollar store. Everything from laundry detergent to doormats can be purchased for one low price. The savings can be significant. Take a look at what you can get from one trip:

- Laundry detergent
- Soap
- Floor cleaner
- Toilet paper
- Paper towels
- Sponges
- Bathroom cleaner
- Glass cleaner
- Air freshener
- Bleach

Ten simple items that you use on a regular basis can be purchased for ten dollars. How much would this cost at any standard grocery store? Around three times as much. A savings of $20 each time you shop can add up. You can buy many other things, but some people are squeamish about food or facial products from the dollar store. I'll leave it up to you, but you can't beat the savings on the basics.

Chapter Lessons

- Learn to be a smart shopper and you can save time, save money, and enhance your quality of life.

- Segmenting your needs and your wants will help you determine what is really important.

Credits and Debits

What can one say about credit cards that hasn't already been said? Even though we know just how dangerous they can be, we still continue to use them. The problem isn't really the cards. It's us. Human nature has a way of taking a good idea and making it bad. A credit card, after all, is a pretty neat idea provided you pay your bills on time. The big problem, however, is that very few people actually do this. And when you don't pay your bills on time, the bills can grow. Secondly, few of us truly understand the terms of our credit cards. The banks that issue the cards prefer not to go out of their way to explain the terms and conditions to you and, instead, choose to bury you in fine print. After all, if they were clear and specific, far fewer people would use them.

In this chapter, we will cover the following topics:

- Credit card components
- Advantages of credit cards
- Disadvantages of credit cards
- To charge or not to charge
- Getting the most out of your credit card
- Fee-based credit cards
- Debit cards
- Credit score 101
- Anatomy of a FICO score

- How to improve your FICO score
- Debunking the myths about FICO scores

Credit Card Components

Consider the key components of a credit card.

Annual Fee

Many credit cards require you to pay an annual fee. My advice is simple—unless you're onstage performing in front of sellout crowds, you're better off avoiding these fees. The fee-based cards entitle you to benefits that can range from discounts on gasoline to your own manservant. Again, my advice is to avoid the fees unless the benefit is truly something you can't live without. The one exception to this might be the cards that offer some sort of rewards benefit such as air miles. If you believe you will accrue enough points to more than offset the fees, then you might consider the card. For example, if the annual fee is $100 and you expect to spend $25,000 per year on the card, you could earn enough points for a free round-trip domestic flight. Assuming that is the case, the card just might make sense.

Late Fee

Most credit cards will charge some sort of late fee. For example, if you miss your payment due date, you could get hit with a fee of $35 or more. It's not the end of the world but, hey, you're not reading this book to learn ways to waste money. To avoid late fees, make sure you set payment reminders on your calendar. Even better, set up an automatic payment plan through your online banking system so that a minimum amount is paid each month. You can always pay any amount over this, but at least this way you will avoid late fees.

Overlimit Fee

This is what you are charged when you exceed your credit card limit. The best part about this if you're a credit card company shareholder is that it can be based on spending, fees, or even finance charges. Suppose you're already behind on your payments and interest charges are piling up. Before long, these charges and late fees could push you over your credit limit. To add insult to injury, you will now be assessed an overlimit fee! To avoid this, make sure you opt out of overlimit processing. Card companies will suggest this as a useful feature but should you sign up for this, be prepared for additional fees. If you opt out (or don't opt in), transactions will be denied when you reach your limit. Better safe than sorry.

Cash Advance Fee

If you use your credit card to withdraw money from an ATM, you will likely be charged a cash advance fee. This could be based on a percentage of the amount you withdraw, which could be up to four percent, or a flat fee. Either way, you will be paying every time. Avoid using the ATM with your credit card and you'll avoid cash advance fees.

Balance Transfer Fee

If you have a credit card, you've probably been inundated by offers for balance transfers. One credit card company offers to pay off the outstanding balance on your existing credit card. If you agree, you have a new credit card and a fresh start. Well, not so fast. You will now pay a balance transfer fee of somewhere between three percent and five percent. That's not necessarily bad if you are transferring balances from a high-interest card to a low-interest card. In other words, if you save more on interest than you spend on the transfer fees, this might make sense. Just make sure you read the fine print because balance transfer offers usually come with teasers such as zero percent interest for the first six months, followed by a jump to a sky-high APR.

Suppose you currently have a $1,000 balance on your credit card and are paying annual interest of 15 percent. Each year, you pay $150 ($1,000 x 15% = $150). A new card offers to transfer the balance for a fee of five percent and zero percent interest for six months. After six months, the rate jumps to 20 percent. Which is better? Assuming you plan on carrying this balance for, say, a year, you would be better off with the transfer. A year on your existing card will cost you $150, but a year on the balance transfer card will cost you the following:

- $50 in fees

- No interest for six months

- Next six months of year ($1,000 x 20% x .5 = $100). After a year, however, the 20 percent annual rate will prove more costly than the old card's 15 percent interest.

The moral to this story is try to pay down balances as soon as possible and, if that proves difficult, consider a balance transfer. Just make sure you pay down the balance before the higher rate kicks in. To compare balance transfer offers, visit http://www.smartbalancetransfers.com/no-transfer-fees/.

Credit Limit

This is the amount you can borrow from or charge off your card. Go over this limit and you could be hit with fees (see above). The bottom line is using up your entire credit line could make it difficult for you to open other accounts, not to mention hurt you credit rating. Should you, however, find yourself reaching your limit, it can't hurt to request a credit limit increase from the credit card company. The worst thing they can do is say no.

Interest Rates

The most important factor in selecting a credit card is the interest rate. Should you carry a balance, this is what you will pay. Avoid credit cards with high interest rates and beware of teaser rates, which usually mean after a period of time, the higher rate kicks in.

Advantages of Credit Cards

Having one or more credit cards is not all bad. A number of advantages present themselves including these pluses:

Rewards. If you spend, you might as well get some perks for your purchases. Airline miles, shopping points, and cash back are just a few of the benefits you earn for using your credit card. For regular spenders, this can pay for more than a few vacations. Just make sure you're not making purchases just to accrue the rewards.

Warranties. This has saved me more than once. Several years ago, a broken laptop was replaced by my credit card company. Thanks, guys!

Flexibility. It's nice to travel the world and not have to carry much, if any, cash. More importantly, it's great not to have to convert one currency to another.

Track spending. One of the greatest features ever. At the end of the month, simply download your statement and you can see exactly what you spent on. Spending too much money will be obvious.

Security. Sure, this really wouldn't be an advantage if you didn't have a credit card, but it's nice to know that if someone steals your card, you can call and cancel it right away. Try doing something similar if someone steals the cash out of your wallet.

Credit score. Without a credit card, your credit score will likely be less than it could be. It's nice to brag that you don't have any debt and you pay for everything with cash. But, in a credit-based economy, demonstrating that you can be a responsible borrower is probably more important, at least as far as the credit bureaus are concerned

Disadvantages of Credit Cards

Interest. No getting around this one. If you carry a balance, you will likely pay dearly.

Late fees. Miss a payment and you'll be hit with fees.

Credit score. Miss a few payments and the fees will pale in comparison to the damage done to your credit score.

Security. No, this is not a mistake. Sure, you can cancel your card if someone steals it, but what if you don't know it has been stolen? Not only are you dealing with someone buying out Walmart, that person just might pretend to be you in many other ways. Unfortunately, credit cards open the door to identity theft.

To Charge or Not to Charge,

That Is the Question

The "Should I keep a credit card?" test:

- Do I pay my bills late?
- Do I enjoy shopping a little too much?
- Do I buy things I don't need often?
- Do I tell my significant other I'm away on business when I'm in Vegas?

Answer yes to any of these? Skip the credit card.

Getting the most out of your credit card

- Set up an automatic payment arrangement with your bank to pay a fixed amount each month.
- Avoid cards that charge an annual fee.
- Avoid carrying a balance.

- Track your spending.
- Track your points.

Fee-Based Credit Cards

The credit card has become a status symbol. Gold, platinum, black—your card reveals your station in life. Flash the platinum card when the check arrives and you're solid. Flash the black card and, well, let's just say that client might invite you back. Membership has its privileges and, of course, its price. Annual fees can run from a few dollars to thousands of dollars. The high-end cards offer an uber-pretentious level of status as well as numerous benefits, which can include concierge services.

So, what's the verdict on fee-based cards? It depends. For example, paying hundreds of dollars a year may make sense for the high-powered business executive who entertains clients and hopscotches from airport to airport. If the card benefits help land business while easing the burdens of the road-warrior lifestyle, perhaps it makes sense. My simple rule of thumb is that your annual credit card fee should not exceed one-tenth of one percent of your annual income. If you earn $100,000 per year, you shouldn't pay more than $100 per year on card fees. Of course, this doesn't mean you have to pay this much. There are plenty of multimillionaires who swear they made their fortunes by avoiding frivolous fees and service charges. So, when choosing a card, consider whether or not the fees justify the personal and financial benefit.

Debit Cards

Debit Card Advantages

Avoid late fees. With a debit card, funds are debited from your bank account when you make a purchase. There are no payments to make because the money is taken out of your account. No payments means no late fees.

Spend what you have (in theory). Since you're not borrowing, you can't really run over budget. The most you'll spend is what you have (unless you have selected the overdraft feature).

Avoid temptation to spend too much. Since it's your own money that you're spending, you will be less inclined to go overboard.

Debit Card Disadvantages

Overdrafts. Like credit cards, you can go over your limit with debit cards, which means overdraft fees. Before long, you're dealing with a credit-card-like scenario (without the benefits of having a credit card).

Account Holds. Imagine this: You're on your dream vacation visiting a pristine tropical island. You decide to rent a scooter for the day and hand the rental agent your debit card. Instead of charging you $100, the rental agent charges $1,000, which includes the scooter rental as well as the security deposit. It gets better. After a day of island exploration, you return the scooter. The charges remain for days even though they were classified as pending authorizations. What does this mean for you? If you head to the ATM to withdraw cash for piña coladas or bobble heads, forget it. The funds will be on hold.

Credit Score 101

Think of personal finance as a recipe. Assets, liabilities, equity, and every concept that supports each of these are like ingredients. If you have the right balance of ingredients, you've made a great dish. Too much of anything and your dish is overwhelmed. The secret sauce that gives the dish just the right kick is the FICO, or credit score. Your FICO score (the name derived from Fair Isaac Corporation who developed it) is a mysterious blend of several ingredients, and it's not entirely clear which of these factors weighs more heavily than others. Most people believe that what affects one person's score may not necessarily affect another person's score. So, why do we bother worrying about the FICO score? For starters, it will determine how much you can borrow and what you pay to borrow. It can also determine whether or not you will receive a loan.

The FICO score is one of the most important determinants of your ability to borrow. Often feared and rarely understood, this simple number can become a life-changing factor. The good news is that it's really up to you in terms of how good you want this number to be. With a little discipline and planning, you can achieve an impressive FICO score.

Anatomy of a FICO Score

The FICO score is so much more than just a simple number. True, the number that appears, ranging from 300 to 850, plays a big role in your financial life. But there's much more behind this number and the credit report that accompanies it. In addition, the report will list whether you've filed for bankruptcy and if there have been any inquiries on your credit recently. Ultimately, creditors will use your score and report to predict your likelihood of default. Specifically, they will consider key components of the report.

Payment History

This part looks at your payment information on various loans including mortgages, credit card loans, auto loans, and so forth. Additionally, it looks for any dark financial clouds hovering above you including bankruptcy, legal judgments, and lawsuits. Finally, it seeks to understand the nature of any delinquencies including specific items that are past due and how long they have been past due.

Balances and Amounts Owed

This component examines the number of accounts that carry balances and what the balances owed are. More specifically, it considers the proportions of credit line balances to credit limits as well as installment loan balances to amounts of original loans. In other words, how much of these borrowing facilities have been paid down.

Length of Credit History

This component looks at the age of the accounts as well as the period of time that has lapsed since recent activity.

New Credit

The number of new accounts opened will play a role as will recent credit inquiries. If you've had credit problems in the past, new accounts and a steady payment record will help.

Types of Credit Used

The different types of credit used play a role in your score.

How to Improve Your FICO Score

Pay your bills on time. Making sure you're up-to-date will not only help avoid any late fees, it will prevent any loss of points.

Keep your outstanding balances low on your credit cards. This will allow you some cushion should you need to borrow more later. If you reach your limit on one or more cards, it brings you one step closer to default, which won't help your score.

Pay off balances when possible. Ah, yes, the first sign of a responsible borrower is the ability to pay off balances. While the credit card companies would prefer you keep balances outstanding, this will help your score as well as your ability to borrow more. If you have overwhelming balances outstanding, work with your creditors to develop a payment plan and pay down that debt!

Keep the number of accounts open to a minimum. It's great to show that you're a responsible borrower, but having too many accounts open, especially ones that are unused, will hurt your score. Find the right balance and, if you have any unused accounts, make sure you close them. Also, try not to keep switching accounts too frequently. FICO likes to see longstanding relationships with creditors and values your loyalty to them.

Have different types of accounts. A diversified portfolio of loans including credit cards, mortgages, auto loans, and student loans will show that you are a solid borrower. I know, it seems counterintuitive to have this kind of debt, but if your balances are reasonable and your payments are on time, you could be a top tier FICO scorer.

Avoid frequent inquiries. If you're comparing loans, do so within a short period of time. Too many credit inquiries over a longer period of time can hurt your score. Doing it within a short span of time keeps it off the FICO radar.

Monitor your score. It pays to stay on top of your score. Being proactive will help you achieve your highest score possible. Contact the credit agency and ask to have late payments more than seven years old as well as any bankruptcies more than seven years old removed from your reports. And make sure any closed accounts do not show up on your report.

A combination of good payment history, a manageable number of accounts, and various debt accounts that have been added over time will give you the right recipe for a solid credit score.

Debunking the Myths about FICO Scores

There is much we do know about credit scores and even more that we don't know. Consider the following myths and you will be better positioned to obtain the best score possible.

Paying your bills on time will shoot your score higher.

Yes and no. You should always do this, but don't expect any major changes. Just as important as paying your bills on time is paying down any balances. And, most of all, consider your credit utilization ratio. This number is based on your credit card balances divided by your total credit limits. According to Kiplinger, you should be using 20 percent or less of your available credit.[1] For example, if you had three credit cards, one with a $5,000 limit and one with a $10,000 limit, your total credit limit would be $15,000. If you have a balance of $3,000, you would be in decent standing as your credit utilization ratio would be 20 percent. If you can pay off some of this, even better, your score should improve. For those of you who are fiscally challenged, an easier option might be to simply ask your credit card companies to increase your lines of credit. This, too, will improve your credit utilization ratio. Just make sure you're not using the increased capacity to spend more!

Closing unused accounts will help your credit score.

Not so fast. Closing unused accounts will only hurt your credit utilization ratio by lowering your overall credit limit. It's especially problematic to do this around the time you're applying for a mortgage or any other significant loans as any major change could affect your ability to obtain the loan or borrow the needed amount.

There is only one all-encompassing credit score.

Wrong. There are several. Equifax, Experian, and TransUnion are the usual suspects and each one offers its own version on just how worthy you really are.

Keeping your credit profile simple is the way to go.

Not quite. While it can give you peace of mind, it won't necessarily help you to build the best credit score possible. It pays to have a little bit of everything to prove to the credit gods that you have what it takes to borrow in every area possible—a mortgage, an auto loan, credit cards, and so on. A strong track record in each area should work wonders for you.

---

[1] Kiplinger, Kimberly Lankford. *Kiplinger Personal Finance.* June 28, 2010.

Chapter Lessons

- Credit cards can help your credit score and offer a good way to track your expenses, but their fees and penalties can be painful.

- Avoid maxing out credit cards and do your best to pay your balances in full.

- Debit cards allow you to spend wisely and stick to a budget.

- Your FICO score is one of the most important things you have and you probably don't realize it.

- Maintaining a fine balance between borrowing and not borrowing too much is a key to achieving a strong credit score.

- Make sure you pay all your bills on time and close unused accounts.

- Monitor your credit score on a regular basis and make sure to contact the credit agencies when problems arise.

Late Night TV and Borrowing

If you're like me, you just might have a weakness for late night TV. Thanks to this vaulted institution, I've managed to acquire a blanket with sleeves, a nose-hair trimmer with a built-in light, and a vacuum-cleaner attachment that cuts hair. And while my next book very well may devote its pages to extolling the virtues of late night infomercial shopping, there is a darker, more insidious side to this pursuit. Sure, there's no denying the myriad lifestyle enhancements associated with these products but, when the products are financial in nature, buyer beware.

It's hard to avoid the charms of washed-up 80s TV stars who peddle everything from reverse mortgages to payday loans at the hour when we are most vulnerable. These infomercials will focus on the innumerable benefits of easy money and the amazing life this creates for you. Unfortunately, they will rarely outline the costs and risks associated with these benefits. As my dad taught me, there's no such thing as a free lunch ... or a free loan.

In this chapter, we'll discuss two topics:

- Predatory lenders
- Types of predatory loans

Predatory Lenders

Predatory lenders are known for catchy phrases to lure you in. Be careful when you hear the following phrases.

Bad credit doesn't matter.

Yes, it does! If you have bad credit, guess what? You need to fix your credit problems before you can borrow. Be careful with lenders who tell you this doesn't matter because what they're really saying is, "Bad credit doesn't matter if you pay us enough." Here's the problem: If you have bad credit, then it's unlikely that you are in any position to pay hefty fees and premiums for a loan. Furthermore, you're probably deeply in debt and taking on more isn't going to help much. Fix your problem first, and then get the loan. Here are reasons why you would ever obtain one of these loans:

- Family member kidnapped
- Led Zeppelin reunion tickets
- Invitation to meet the real Bigfoot
- Crown jewels for sale on eBay

We'll help you refinance later.

Sure you will. And you'll buy me a vacation home, put my kids through college, give me a job ... Why stop there? They can promise you anything but, in reality, even if they deliver, it comes at a price.

We have the lowest rates around.

For now. Rates can easily soar higher assuming the loan is based on an adjustable rate so be very careful with teaser rates. If they seem too good to be true, well ...

I know a guy who knows a guy ...

Sure, brokers can do a lot of the legwork for you but, keep in mind, someone is paying them and ultimately those fees are borne by you. So, while they might get you a good deal, you probably would have gotten a better deal on your own.

Predatory Loan Types

There are a number of different loan types that may seem OK at first, but on second glance, steer clear.

Payday loans

These nifty funding mechanisms are basically short-term loans secured by the borrower's next paycheck. Here's the big problem with payday loans: Because they are short-term and the interest is often quoted on a two-week term, the effective annual rate (EAR) can be substantial. For example, if you take out a loan for $200 and pay a $20 fee for a two-week loan, you are basically paying ten percent. The annual percentage rate would be substantially higher (26 weeks x 10% = 260%).

Here's how it works. You go to a store in a neighborhood usually adorned with kettledrum fires. You approach a weathered sign that reads "Fast Cash." Inside, a man behind bulletproof glass greets you with a gilded smile. You present some type of employment verification or income verification (maybe a paystub or bank statement) and write a post-dated check in the full amount of the loan plus any associated fees. The guy with the gold teeth hands you the cash for the loan amount, holds onto your check, and, on the maturity date, you're expected to return to the store and pay back the loan. If you don't return, the guy may cash your check. If, for some reason, the check bounces or your account is short of funds, you face fees and penalties from your bank. Meanwhile, your loan remains outstanding and interest continues to accrue. In other words, you're in big trouble.

Here is the problem with payday loans. They are often criticized for catering to low-income people, many of whom already have bad credit. The interest rates are exorbitant and, given the dire financial circumstances of many borrowers, a bad situation becomes worse. The flip side of this is that the default rate is high and, therefore, the lenders must charge the hefty fees. And many argue (usually the owners of the lending shops) that they offer a quick source of liquidity to their customers. So, what's my take on this, you ask? Well, you can make a case for these loans, so the best advice is be careful. They should be treated as a lender of last resort. Think of yourself as a distressed bank and the payday lender as a great big government TARP program. They may bail you out, but you will pay dearly for it.

Single Premium Credit Insurance

This type of insurance offers the advantage of paying off a loan in case you, the homebuyer, dies. My simple question is, "Who cares?" You'll be dead and clearly facing more important things to contend with. Sure, you can make the argument that this protects your next of kin, but my suggestion is if you care enough about them to protect them, take out a good life insurance policy. The major problem with single-premium credit insurance is the hefty premiums due to the fact that there is no health-exam requirement. You might be the picture of perfect health, but you will very likely pay a premium associated with someone about to breathe his last breath. Additionally, the premiums are often baked into the loan itself so it's difficult to see how much you're actually paying. Be careful.

Overdraft Loans

Many banks offer what is affectionately titled "Overdraft Protection," which is anything but protection. Sure, this allows you to withdraw more money than you actually have, but this comes at a steep price. The interest on overages can be exorbitant and very rarely are you notified that you've overdrawn. Since so few of us check our bank balances on a daily basis, this can cause you to rack up hefty fees. Suppose your bank account has a balance of $1,000. You just wrote a check for $500 that you forget about. The check was cashed and your balance is now $500. You go to the ATM and withdraw $600. The ATM dispenses the $600 meaning you're overdrawn by $100. The bank charges you $25 as a one-time overdraft fee. Additionally, the bank may charge you an additional fee for each day your account remains overdrawn! That $100 loan may soon be substantially higher. Many banks offer this protection whether you know it or not. If you can opt out of it, you should. No sense borrowing a few bucks without knowing you've actually borrowed. And if you choose to keep it, make sure you check your balances on a regular basis and be mindful of every check you write, every debit card purchase, and every ATM withdrawal.

Title Loans

Not unlike payday loans, these nifty products require you to post the title to your beloved vehicle as collateral. If you can't pay off the loan on time, guess who won't be driving that sweet ride. To avoid this tragic fate, the loan provider is kind enough to keep you apprised of your status and, when you're behind on your payments, they demand you pay the hefty interest on the loan to stop them from taking your vehicle. This is a strong incentive to keep paying these charges and, unfortunately, it can lead to a perpetual cycle of simply paying the interest without making any headway on the principal. And the worse-case scenario is you can no longer make the interest payments, meaning you lose your car and possibly your only means of transportation to work.

Refund Anticipation Loans

Who doesn't like getting free money? Well, no one, but unfortunately it doesn't really exist. And while refund anticipation loans may appear to be just that on the surface, they can prove costly. These loans are offered by tax preparers who basically give you the money that you should receive based on your tax refund. Instead of waiting several months for the money, you get it at the time your return is completed. The only problem is that a hefty fee is tied to this so while you avoid waiting a few months to receive your money from Uncle Sam, you pay dearly for it. Avoid this expensive form of cash advance unless the alternative is a broken kneecap.

Reverse Mortgages

Every time I see an infomercial about reverse mortgages, I'm astonished by how adept the spokesperson is at avoiding discussion of what a reverse mortgage really is. He never describes the structure nor does he outline the factors that you should be aware of when considering one. Instead, the discussion focuses on how much it will make your life better. Reverse mortgages offer you the ability to convert your home's equity into cash. Unfortunately, it can erase a lifetime's worth of paying principal and property appreciation. In other words, your entire home is owned by someone else if you opt for a reverse mortgage. That may not be so bad if you need the cash and place little conceptual value on home ownership. After all, perhaps it's better to have money in your pocket than money tied up in a home—money that you may never see. So, while I and many others are not necessarily against the idea of reverse mortgages, I do believe the companies that offer them need to be clear on what the borrower is actually involved in. The fees can be significant and most borrowers are oblivious to these fees. The amount of money available to the consumer is determined by five primary factors:

- The appraised value of the property
- Any repairs needed on the house
- Any liens on the house
- Interest rate to be determined by the U.S. Treasury T-Bill or LIBOR index
- The age of the homeowner. Usually, the older the homeowner, the larger the loan amount

The payment terms are worth considering when deciding on a reverse mortgage. A line of credit, a lump sum, or monthly installments are the three common payment options available to a reverse mortgage holder. A line of credit will offer the most money and the lump sum offers cash immediately. Monthly installments can be the most advantageous provided the interest payments are reasonable.

Chapter Lessons

- Avoid predatory lenders by learning the tools of their trade.

- Always read the fine print and understand all fees.

- Be particularly cautious of extraordinarily high-interest loans that offer easy money.

Financing a Home

Let's imagine that you start a business—we'll call it a dry-cleaning business—and all of a sudden the business takes off and you decide it's time to move on up to, say, a deluxe apartment in the sky. This represents the chance to live in a nice home and make new friends. Compelling, right? However, this new apartment comes with a hefty price tag and deciding how to finance it will become a major challenge, along with managing your soon-to-be neighbors.

In Chapter 2, we introduced the concept of a liability and what it means in terms of your personal balance sheet. One of the most important liabilities and one that you will very likely assume at some point, if you haven't already, is a mortgage. A mortgage can help you achieve what many believe to be an integral part of the American dream—homeownership. While there is still considerable debate whether homeownership is a right or privilege, the fact is that it's not going away and many of us will contemplate it at some point. And if contemplation becomes a reality, chances are a mortgage will play a role.

When you buy a home, it's more than likely that a significant portion of the purchase price will be covered by a mortgage. It's rare that you would pay cash for your home and, even if you could afford to, you would likely still finance it with a mortgage assuming the mortgage terms are favorable. Herein lies the problem with mortgages. While most homeowners have them, few understand their terms. And that's exactly what the banks want. By keeping you oblivious to the terms and structures of mortgages, you are more likely to assume one without understanding exactly what you're getting yourself into. Remember, not all mortgages are created equal. The more you know, the more you'll save.

In this chapter, we'll talk about these issues:

- What to consider when applying for a mortgage

- Mortgage refinancing

- Fannie and Freddie Who?

- Why homeownership is not for everyone

- The case for renting

What to Consider When Applying for a Mortgage

When you apply for a mortgage, it is important that you brush up on all relevant concepts and ask some very important key questions. To start, make sure you're ready to fire off the following ones.

What Is the Rate?

Interest is the amount you pay on your outstanding balance. The number is usually quoted as an annual rate but calculated on a monthly basis. Suppose your annual interest rate is quoted at six percent. Your monthly rate will actually be 0.5 percent. Mortgages are generally a fixed rate, meaning the interest doesn't change, or an adjustable rate, meaning the interest can vary depending on fluctuations in some interest rate index. The beauty of adjustable rate mortgages is that the interest rate risk is transferred from the lender to the borrower. In other words, you have to stress about shifts in macroeconomic indicators while the lender sleeps well at night. Of course, when interest rates drop, it's nice to have an adjustable rate mortgage. In the end, having an adjustable rate mortgage is best suited to the Vegas and Atlantic City regulars. If leaving your fate to chance is your thing, than perhaps you have the intestinal fortitude to endure an adjustable rate mortgage.

What Is the Term?

Five, ten, fifteen, thirty years … take your pick. Do you want to pay it off sooner or later? Do you need lower monthly payments in exchange for a higher rate or higher monthly payments and a longer duration in exchange for a lower rate? There's really no right answer here. It simply depends on whether you need cash in your pocket today and what you plan to do with that cash. In order to decide on the right term, you have to decide on a monthly payment that you would be comfortable with.

What Is the Down Payment

This is the amount of the home purchase price that you will pay at the time of purchase from your own funds. Pay a little and you're borrowing more, which means heftier monthly payments. Pay a lot and you're borrowing less and making lighter monthly payments.

What Is the Mortgage Size?

The cost of the home minus the down payment will roughly equal the mortgage amount (the amount you borrow).

What Determines the Monthly Payments

The interest rate, mortgage term, and mortgage amount will determine how much you pay each month.

The Case for a Shorter-Term Mortgage

A shorter term will usually mean a higher monthly payment. The flip side is that your interest rate will be lower and, in the end, you will end up paying less in total interest. If you are adamant about giving the bank as little as possible, this is the way to go. The challenge for you, however, will be cash flow each month. With higher monthly payments, you will have less money left over at the end of each month to spend on other things. If that is not a problem, this just might be the way to go. And, most of all, you will become a mortgage-free homeowner a lot sooner with a shorter-term mortgage. Owning a home without any debt attached to it is truly something to be proud of.

The Case for a Longer-Term Mortgage

A longer term will usually mean a lower monthly payment but a higher interest rate. This makes sense if stronger cash flow is important to you. If having more money to spend on other things besides a mortgage at the end of the month is a priority for you, this is the way to go. Over the life of the mortgage, however, you will pay more in interest than you would for a shorter-term mortgage. So, while you pay more over time, you also have more money in your pocket each month. If you plan to live in your home for a long time, this may not be the best scenario. You could end up giving away a good portion of what would otherwise amount to your life savings to the bank.

The Process

Applying for a mortgage is not what it used to be. During the housing boom, applying for a mortgage was akin to buying a carton of milk. Nowadays, it's more like securing a job with the CIA. Banks will ask for just about any piece of information they can conceive of and, chances are, they'll ask for it even after you've given it to them. The pendulum effect of the mortgage business has made banks extra cautious and, as such, every borrower is assumed to be a mortgage deadbeat. My advice, if you apply for a mortgage, is to try not to blame the banks for these inevitable hassles. They're doing what they can to prevent another system wide failure. Be prepared to produce the required documentation and understand a bit about what they're basing their approval decision on.

FICO Score

Clearly, a good credit score is needed to secure a mortgage. Anything less than good won't necessarily be a deal breaker but can drive up the cost of your mortgage. Make sure you pay your bills on time and avoid late fees and penalties.

Debt-to-Income Ratio

If you're cool enough to be a mortgage industry insider, you call this the DTI, which is calculated based on your monthly debt payments divided by your monthly gross, or pre-tax, income. The lower the number, the better the indication of stronger capacity to cover your debt service. Debt payments will include mortgage payments as well as other payments such as student loan payments, car loan payments, and credit card payments. Additionally, legal judgments, child support payments, and alimony payments will be included as well. Here's how it works:

Suppose your annual gross income is $48,000. Your monthly gross income would be $4,000 ($48,000 divided by 12). If the bank requires a debt-to-income ratio of 40 percent, you would only be able to carry monthly debt payments of no more than $1,600 ($4,000 x .4 = $1,600). In other words, $1,600 is the most allowed for you mortgage and related costs plus other recurring debt. If the mortgage payments themselves are $1,600 and you have auto loan payments, you're out of luck. The bank will not approve your mortgage until either your monthly debt payments fall under $1,600 or your income increases.

Source of Funds

From where will the funds come from to make your down payment? Hopefully, you have enough in your bank account to cover this. Additionally, it's good to have at least twice your monthly mortgage payment held as reserve. This will make the mortgage underwriter feel more secure about your application.

Property Value

The appraised value or purchase price of the property is an important consideration in the mortgage property. It drives another important ratio, which is the LTV, or loan-to-value, ratio. When you divide the total mortgage amount by the property value, you come up with the LTV ratio. Banks will look at this number to make sure the loan is not too large for the property. For example, if the mortgage is expected to be $200,000 and the property is valued at $250,000, the LTV will be 80 percent. If the bank has a limit on LTV of 75 percent, chances are your mortgage application will be denied. At that point, your best option would be to ask for a smaller mortgage, which means more money down.

Mortgage Refinancing

These days, it's hard to ignore the compelling case for mortgage refinancing. With rates hovering near all-time lows, the financial benefits of such a move abound. At the very least, refinancing can save you a sizeable amount over the life of your loan. However, the monthly savings must be measured against the costs associated with refinancing.

Specifically, it's important to consider all up-front fees and closing costs associated with the new loan. This often includes up-front points (a percentage of the loan amount), application fees, title insurance, transfer fees, taxes, and appraisals to name a few. It's not uncommon for these fees to reach several thousand dollars for a conventional loan. The bank will often build these fees into the loan principal, which means all you see is the lower monthly payments. Be careful because while you pay less each month, you could end up paying more in total over the life of the loan or while you own your home.

Why Refinance?

Lower interest rate. Pretty simple here. The interest you pay on your mortgage principal is your cost of the mortgage. If you can get a better rate, your cost goes down. Lowering your rate by even one-half percent can lower your interest payments and your overall monthly payments by hundreds of dollars for a conventional mortgage. That is money in your pocket and a potential lifestyle enhancer. Imagine saving $200 per month. In the course of a year, the $2,400 you save could pay for a nice overseas vacation. Not bad for a little paperwork.

Build equity faster. Refinancing allows you to pay more toward principal and, in turn, build your equity faster. In other words, you will own your home sooner rather than later. A lower interest payment or shorter-term mortgage will help you reach homeowner Nirvana sooner rather than later.

Change mortgage type (ARM to fixed). If you opted for an adjustable rate mortgage (ARM), things look pretty good provided interest rates continue to drop. Unfortunately, if they rise, you're on the hook for the increases. If you sense that increases are forthcoming, it's in your best interest to refinance into a fixed rate mortgage. Of course, if you're already in a fixed rate mortgage and rates continue to drop, perhaps an ARM is the right choice. Of course, there is no right way to do this and unless you have the ability to predict the future, this is little more than a bet. Nonetheless, it just might be a bet worth taking.

Cash out. Refinancing usually involves an appraisal of some sort. If your property is appraised at a higher value than what you paid for it, it's quite possible that you may be able to borrow more than the principal amount outstanding. This means you can swap into a new mortgage and have money left over to spend on other things. Be careful with this, however. At the end of the day, these are still borrowed funds and, if you decide to take your newly acquired treasure to the mall, your tactics are scarcely different from maxing out the AmEx.

Being Ready to Refinance

Always keep paystubs, tax returns, brokerage statements, and other income statements.

So, what should you consider in order to make a mortgage refinancing worth your while?

1. Make sure the rate is low enough that the interest savings will cover any closing costs within a short amount of time, say, 24 months.

2. Negotiate with the bank to bring down the closing costs. You may have more pull with the bank that holds your existing mortgage.

3. Avoid looking at the reduction in monthly payments and focus on the overall interest savings. This will benefit you in the long run.

Fannie and Freddie Who?

Weren't they characters in a Swedish film? Chocolatiers? Apparently, they are government-sponsored enterprises that are designed to expand the secondary mortgage market. Fannie Mae is also known as Federal National Mortgage Association and Freddie Mac is also known as Federal Home Loan Mortgage Corporation. These two organizations buy the mortgages from banks so that the banks have more money to make more loans. Seems like a noble cause, right? So, why does any of this matter to you? Well, Fannie and Freddie make homeownership affordable. If they continue to buy the loans from the banks, the banks continue to lend to homebuyers at reasonable rates. So, in essence, everyone wins. The banks win because they make more loans and make more money. Fannie and Freddie win because they buy the loans and repackage them into nifty financial instruments that go up in value, and you win because you get to take out a mortgage at a decent rate. But one thing I've learned about everyone-wins scenarios is that they can easily become everyone-loses scenarios. At the height of the financial crisis, the loans that Fannie and Freddie held were dropping in value as the underlying home values that they were based on dropped in value. This meant that both companies were on the verge of collapse and, as such, sent mortgage lenders into a tailspin. If Fannie and Freddie collapsed, who would buy the mortgages issued by these banks?

Why Homeownership Is Not for Everyone

With the housing crash of 2008–2009, the myth that buying your own home was the key to prosperity was dealt a severe blow. Lets look at reasons why homeownership may not be best for you.

Financial Risk

The financial crisis taught us an important lesson: Home prices do not always go higher. A family friend once remarked at the height of the housing boom, "Why don't you buy a house?" I responded, "I don't need the added burden or expense of homeownership. Plus, I like my apartment." "Just buy a house and sell it next year. You will make money because home prices always appreciate." Hmmm. That's what many of us thought for quite some time but, unfortunately, we learned a rather painful lesson when the housing market crashed a few years back. The reality, in fact, is that home prices are not unlike prices on many other assets in that they can go up and they can just as easily go down. That being said, if you buy a home at a reasonable price, you might see some appreciation. Consider this along with the other costs and hassles of homeownership before you take the plunge.

Costs

It's not just the mortgage payments. It's insurance, taxes, utilities, and maintenance. These expenses can add up and, if you're already stretched financially, these costs could make matters worse. You can always downsize to a smaller apartment, but moving to a smaller home can be a major hassle and cause you to incur additional expense.

Foreclosure

Miss a few payments and the bank can take over your home. Not only do you lose your abode, but your credit rating and equity in the home will be lost forever. Miss a few rent payments on an apartment and, while not ideal, you get evicted. All in all, a better option than losing your home that you bought with your hard-earned money.

Mobility

Again, it's easier to move from a rental than an owned property. Job relocation is a fact of life and should the job as head of paper-supply procurement in Toledo beckon you, it may be difficult if you are stuck in your home.

The Case for Renting

Think about a world in which you have few obligations and few financial burdens. Chances are, in that world, you rent an apartment. No mortgage, no interest payments, no property taxes, no property insurance. Just the simple pleasure of coming home to a place that's not really yours. Each month you make your rent payments, you have a place to stay. Stop making the payments and you might be sleeping in the bus depot.

Limited financial risk. With no money down and no hefty monthly payments, you're simply on the hook for your rent. The real estate market can collapse and guess what—you still sleep well at night.

Mobility. If you decide to leave, no problem. You might lose your security deposit and few months rent, but that pales in comparison to the cost of trying to move on a moment's notice when you own a home.

Opportunity. Not owning a home can leave the door open for opportunity. A new business venture, a vacation, a nice car, a college education—these are all things you will have an easier time paying for if you don't have a small fortune tied up in your house. Don't take my word for it. Ask any of the folks who live in million-dollar mansions and still stop at thrift stores. A mortgage has a way of eating up a nice chunk of your disposable income. There's a reason why it's called being "house poor."

Great parties! It's an apartment and should you feel the urge to party like a rock star, well, let's just say I'd rather put a hole in someone else's wall than my own wall.

Chapter Lessons

- Careful planning and financial organization will help facilitate a smooth mortgage application process.

- Refinancing a mortgage can save you money in the short run as well as the long run. Just make sure you understand all the terms associated with the refinancing process and new loan.

- Homeownership may very well be part of the American Dream, but it doesn't mean it's for everyone. Make sure you understand the liabilities and responsibilities associated with being a homeowner before you decide to become one.

Buying a Car

Here's the skinny on buying a car. I realize that nearly every personal finance book out there will tell you that buying a car is the worst financial commitment you'll ever make. Cars depreciate fast and consume significant resources due to use and maintenance. Yet we all dream of one day owning the noisy muscle car (I do, at least), the Italian sportster, or the tricked-out minivan with 12 DVD players. So, should you skip the car altogether? If you don't have the money for one, perhaps. But if you can afford a car and need one for your job, you should consider getting one.

Many of us pay more attention to our cars than our immediate family members. And while that may sometimes be justified, it says a good deal about us as a culture. We love our cars. Not only do they get us from point A to point B, they serve as an alter ego. They provide us with shelter, comfort, even entertainment. And, for many of us, this may be the largest purchase we ever make. I won't tell you whether you should drive a car or not, and I certainly won't offer my insights on greenhouse emissions and global warming. I'll simply do my best to guide you through the financing mechanisms involved with car ownership. In this chapter, we'll cover two topics related to purchasing a car:

- Leasing vs. buying a car
- Tips for buying a car

Leasing vs. Buying a Car

This burning question has consumed humankind since the dawn of civilization or at least for the last few years. To be honest, there is no clear answer. It really depends on several factors:

How long you plan to drive the car. The general rule here is if you still wear polyester slacks, chances are you drive your cars into the ground. If that is the case, you'd better buy the car because a lease could prove expensive. While many dealers will allow you to buy the car after the lease term is up, chances are you will be paying a premium for a now-used car.

How many miles you expect to drive the car per year? Most leases come with strict mileage restrictions. Exceed these limits and you're in store for some hefty overage charges. If you log a fair amount of miles each year, it will likely make more sense to buy.

Who is paying for the car? If your company reimburses you for your car, let them make the lease payments, which will likely give you the opportunity to change cars every few years.

If it will be for business use or personal use. If you're a business owner and you use the car for business, your monthly lease payments can be deducted for tax purposes as a business expense.

Why You Should Lease

One of the biggest advantages of leasing is that you don't have to plunk down piles of money to lease. You can retain your cash and invest it elsewhere. Your monthly payments may prove to be relatively low on a lease, which can improve your monthly cash flow. This is particularly helpful if you have other expenses to tackle or other financial opportunities to pursue. And, best of all, you can swap your car for another with relative ease when your lease is up. If you embrace change and like new toys, this could be the ideal scenario for you.

Why You Shouldn't Lease

If you're leaning toward leasing a car, consider the equity issue. When you buy a car, you own something. If you lease a car, you own nothing. At the end of the lease, you've spent a lot of money and have nothing to show for it. In a way, it's similar to renting an apartment or owning a house. Owning an asset will give you some residual value while leasing or renting will simply drain your resources. That's not always bad, but it is certainly something you'll want to consider. Additionally, leases come with rules and restrictions. If that's your thing, a lease might be right for you. But if you like to march to the beat of your own drum, this can be oppressive. Suppose you decide to hightail it for a cross-country road trip with your buddies for a weekend. Better reconsider or take the bus. The extra mileage on your car could cause you to accrue charges of up to 15 cents per each mile above your annual limit! That could prove a very expensive Vegas trip, and we're not even factoring in all the pricey pursuits that Vegas has to offer. And forget about ending your lease early. This comes with all kinds of wonderful penalties. Lastly, be careful how you drive. Chances are your insurance will only cover the market value of the car if you total it. This may not cover you for whatever balance you owe on the lease, which could be more.

Why You Should Buy

Car ownership is a source of pride for many people, but aside from that, there can be some economic advantages as well. The key to whether it makes sense to own a car rests in depreciation. In other words, you have to determine how long you will keep the car and how much it will be worth when you sell it. For example, if your dream car costs $20,000 new and you hope to keep it for five years, how much will it be worth at that time? Tough question to answer, but you can estimate the value based on older models that sell today. Let's assume that after five years, your car will be worth around $10,000. This means you spent $10,000 to drive it for five years, or $2,000 per year, or $167 per month. Compare this to the cost of leasing the same car for five years. If monthly payments on the lease are more, then the purchase makes more sense. Here's where it gets complicated. The cash involved in purchasing the car can be substantial and, while your total expense during the time you own the car may be less than the lease, the opportunity cost of owning the car could be significant. If you paid cash for your car, you gave up $20,000 that could have been used for something else. Sure, you expect to receive $10,000 of it back in five years, but you've tied up the money for a long time. Suppose that money could have been used to start a side business. You may have given up an opportunity worth far more than a few thousand dollars. In the end, buying a car vs. leasing a car will come down to monthly payments and opportunity cost. If buying the car is the lower-cost option and there is no opportunity cost associated with it, the choice is clear: Buy the car.

Why You Shouldn't Buy

This one shouldn't be too hard to figure out. First of all, a car depreciates faster than most assets. Drive it for a few years and it's worth a mere fraction of what you paid for it. At the same time, you're paying every year for maintenance, which, depending on the type of car you buy, can be substantial. And, finally, insurance doesn't come cheap. So, unless you really need a car or derive some serious enjoyment from driving one, it might make sense to avoid buying one.

Ride Share

One of the best concepts to surface over the last few years is the ride share. Budget-conscious drivers can pay a fraction of what they would pay to drive a car and have that car when they need it. The easiest way to go about this is to join one of the many ride-share programs in your area. For a nominal monthly fee and an hourly rate, you can usually take a car out when you need to. A more complex option is to partner with some friends and buy a car together. Just make sure to clearly define the usage terms and allocation of costs before getting involved in something like this. If done in haste, you could find yourself without a car and without friends.

Tips for Buying a Car

Ideally, buy a car that reflects your personality. Going too far overboard makes you look pretentious and can fuel jealousy. Being exceptionally modest and going with the old Gremlin makes you look sloppy and excessively tight. My view is this: Buy the car befitting of someone in the next job you hope to have. Most of all, make sure you can afford it. And, keep it clean. A messy car is a messy mind and, when your friends and colleagues see this, it will reflect poorly on you.

From a financial standpoint, the best option I can recommend is a slightly used car with full warranty. I know the new-car smell is great, but thanks to the wonders of late night infomercials; you can buy that smell in a can. The beauty of a nearly new car is that it has already depreciated substantially yet it performs and looks brand-new. Buy one with a full warranty and you are covered for nearly any major problem. And, best of all, you can easily save 20 percent off the price of a comparable new car. Now, if paying full price for the new-car smell and thrill of being the first person to drive it is worthwhile, go for it. I'm not one to judge and, while I enjoy spreading the used-car gospel, no one in my immediate family has ever followed my advice. They insist on buying brand-new. Perhaps that says less about my views and more about the kind of respect I command in my family.

Financing a Car Purchase

Financing a car can be a good option if you're cash-strapped and the terms are favorable. The dealer may offer you financing, which is convenient but that convenience usually comes at a price as the rate may be higher and payments could be front-loaded, meaning you pay more interest up front. If you pay off the loan early, you're clearly paying more than you need to be. Banks can offer better rates, but you will likely have to wait a few days for approval and may end up filling out more paperwork.

Rates

The dealer will try everything possible to get you to buy the car and get you to finance it through the dealer. The financing arm of the dealer can be more profitable than the sales arm. Dealers often mark up the interest on your loan above the rate quoted by the dealer's lender. This is standard practice and you should assume it to be the case. Usually, newer cars will have lower rates as will longer-term car loans. With this in mind, it doesn't hurt to ask for a lower rate. The worst thing the dealer can say is no.

Ready for Battle

Let's face it. Buying a car is war, and you have to be ready for battle. Car dealers are in the business of making money, and it's up to you to protect yourself from paying more than you have to. Your singular goal is to drive a car home that cost you as little as possible. Here's what you need to do:

Know your credit score. This will help you better understand your prospects for good loan terms should you choose to finance.

Know the value of your existing car. Visit Kelly Blue Book at www.kbb.com to get an idea what your trade-in value would be.

Know your budget. Knowing how much you can afford will save you time and hassle when it comes time to finalize your options.

Know the incentives. Go to the dealer's web site as well as the manufacturer's web site to learn about all rebates and low-interest financing incentives.

Know the competition. Shop around and find out what other dealers are willing to offer for similar cars. This will help your bargaining position when it comes time to make your final offer.

Chapter Lessons

- It pays to understand the pros and cons of buying as well as leasing a car.
- While there is no easy answer, look for the option best suited to your needs.

- Consider other options, such as ride sharing, which can be economical if you don't drive frequently.

- Should you choose to buy a car, make sure you come prepared to the dealer.

12

Financing an Education

I don't want to sell anything, buy anything, or process anything as a career. I don't want to sell anything bought or processed, or buy anything sold or processed, or process anything sold, bought, or processed, or repair anything sold, bought, or processed. You know, as a career, I don't want to do that.

—Lloyd Dobler, *Say Anything*

Paying for an education is something the majority of us will have to contend with at some point. Whether it's your own education or your kid's education, education requires smart financial planning. There are few freebies these days so we just have to accept the responsibility. Some of you are getting ready for school and others have long since left it behind but, if you're like many people these days, you're still paying for it. Better get used to it and better stay on top of it because if you don't, well, look out below. Financing an education can be daunting and knowing where to begin can be the toughest part. Four years of school can cost between $40,000 and $200,000, which can be more than the price of, or at least the down payment on, a home. While a home may increase in value, an education is difficult to value in financial terms. Plan for school just as ardently as you plan for your retirement and you will minimize a great deal of anxiety and stress. If I've scared you, well, good. That's the idea. I see far too many people approach this lightly only to find themselves trying to market a degree in underwater basket weaving to a major investment bank. Consider the outlined steps and you will avoid hassles, allowing you to focus on what really counts—getting the best education possible.

In this chapter, we will discuss three topics:

- Planning for an education
- Funding sources
- Free Application for Federal Student Aid (FAFSA)

Planning for an Education

In order to plan for your education, it's important that you take the following steps to ensure you're on the right path to managing the cost of school. Grab your parents, grab your kids. This is a family affair, and it's important that everyone with a vested interest in it is involved.

Start saving. This begins as soon as you stop spending more than you earn. Whether you're the parent of a newborn, or a teenager with your first job, or both (in which case you and your kid just might go to college at the same time), you should start saving. Any simple, risk-free, interest-bearing account will do, although don't expect your money to grow significantly. Better options might be education savings accounts (ESAs) and Section 529 plans. These government-sponsored plans allow you to invest money without paying taxes on the earnings as long as you use the money for school. Any unused money that you withdraw, of course, will be taxed. Not a bad way to save for college and you can't beat the tax savings.

Determine how much your school of choice will cost. Choose the most expensive school you think you or your child will likely attend and start budgeting for it. If you have no idea what school that will be, err on the side of excess and budget for an expensive school.

Attend financial aid seminars hosted by the school. As college approaches, it's always helpful to gain insights straight from the source.

Pinpoint sources of funding. Consider every possible source available and don't rule anything out. Apply for everything available and do it early.

Work out a budget to cover any out-of-pocket expenses. Once you've received word from your school and your aid money is determined, make sure you have a budget in place to cover your out-of-pocket expenses. Hopefully, you've saved as much as possible but, even then, you will likely need to cover some of the expenses from your earnings.

Funding Sources

Grants

Grants are financial awards given to help students finance their education. These awards tend to be need-based more than merit-based so it's up to you to present your or your family's financial capacity. There's no magical formula to determine need when it comes to qualifying for a grant, but chances are if you struggle to make ends meet, you're probably a good candidate. Make sure you explore every available grant, no matter how small or how rigorous the application process. Every penny counts here. Grant sources include federal, state, and local governments; community organizations; schools; private companies; unions; and nonprofits. The most important lesson here is to apply early. The early bird catches the worm and that is definitely true here. Once the money is spent on someone else, it's not coming your way.

Student Loans

So, this is the one we all hope to avoid because, like everything else, it comes at a price. And it's a price we just might end up paying for the rest of our lives. The problem with student loans is twofold:

1. We rarely think about what it will actually cost us in the end.

2. We blindly assume that because we have an education, we will earn enough to pay off our loans.

Ignoring the cost of loans and making this assumption can be very dangerous. Just ask any of my friends who assumed six-figure debt loads but will likely see a man on Mars before their loans are paid off. I strongly encourage you to do everything you can to finance your education through every other means possible and think of student loan agencies as the lender of last resorts. Clearly, most of us will need to borrow some portion of our education costs, but knowing what you are getting yourself into is just as important as determining how much to borrow. Here is what you need to know about student loans:

Subsidized loans. The federal government pays the interest while the student is in school.

Expected family contribution. The EFC is what your family is expected to pay. Calculating this will involve your family's total income, assets and benefits, family size, and the number of family members who will attend school during the year.

Grace period. The period of time you are given before you have to start paying back your loans. Normally, the grace period is six months for a federal Stafford Loan and nine months for a federal Perkins Loan.

Deferment. This is a temporary period during which you are not required to make payments on your student loans. During this time, the government pays the interest on subsidized loans and the borrower pays the interest on unsubsidized loans.

Forbearance. If you don't qualify for deferment, try forbearance, which allows borrowers to temporarily postpone payments or make smaller ones.

Independent student. To qualify for independent student status, you must meet one of the following criteria: be at least 24 years old, a graduate or professional student, a veteran, a member of the armed forces, married, an orphan, a ward of the court, or someone with legal dependents.

Dependent student. If you don't qualify for any of the items listed above, you're likely a dependent student.

Repayment schedule. This schedule tells you when your loan payments are due along with the term of the loan. Federal loans offer the choice of more than one repayment plan depending on the type of the loan. Standard repayment plans will likely require you to pay a fixed amount each month for up to ten years to pay the loan back.

Scholarships

Scholarships are similar to grants but tend to be more merit-based. Criteria are typically based on academic, artistic, or athletic achievement. More obscure scholarships are awarded based on candidates' duck-calling abilities or proficiency in Klingon. Research every available scholarship—you never know.

Loans

Like most forms of debt, loans must be repaid to the lender. The U.S. Department of Education and private lenders offer various student loans. Perkins and Stafford Loans tend to be popular federal loan programs. Private lenders may offer flexible terms but at higher rates. Always review interest rates, payment schedules, and origination fees when comparing loans. When you graduate, consider consolidating your loans, which could lower your interest payments. Never borrow more than you need!

Work-Study

Working part-time during school can save you huge loan payments down the road. This can be the area in which you have most control. Most schools will offer well-paying, part-time jobs to financial aid recipients. Working while in school can offer you a much-needed break from academics. But don't overdo it—you're there to study!

Managing Student Loans

When I was a kid, I always believed that financing an education was the closest thing to free money. I learned that this was clearly not the case when I finished college and found myself drowning in debt. Seven years later, I was finishing business school in the midst of a recession and facing the harsh reality of serious debt payments. Being several hundred thousand dollars in debt and having no job, I did what any reasonable person would do—I partied like a rock star. I spent my afternoons in the gym, evenings napping, and nights doing unspeakable things at underground clubs. In the end, this left me with a very important lesson: Debt sucks. And it rarely goes away. And you can run from it, but you can't hide from it. And hangovers can't be cured. So, I regrouped and started to rebuild my life with a goal in mind: Get rid of my student loan debt. I was able to do this by following a few steps:

* Consolidate loans
* Determine which loans have the highest interest
* Determine if the interest is variable or fixed
* Start paying down principal

Free Application for Federal Student Aid (FAFSA)

The FAFSA is one of the most important forms you will ever fill out. Students or parents can submit this form annually to determine eligibility for student financing. Make sure you follow these important tips to maximize your chances of receiving financial aid.

Do not procrastinate. Get going ASAP. The longer you wait, the more likely you are to make errors, or worse, miss the deadline for submission. If you don't have exact or complete tax form numbers, you can fill out the FAFSA form that allows you to submit estimated numbers.

Do not include equity. FAFSA doesn't inquire if you own your home or rent it so no need to mention this nor should you mention other fixed assets.

Do not mention retirement holdings. 401Ks, IRAs, and other retirement plans need not be mentioned. If you are feeling generous and decide to share this information, it could drastically hurt your chances of getting financial aid.

Proofread everything. Make sure you double- and triple-check items for errors and, even after you have submitted the form, you can go online and correct errors.

Pell Grants

Pell Grants offer need-based grants to low-income families. This is one of the greatest things the government has ever done, and you should explore this option to see if you qualify. Grant consideration is based on the following:

- Overall expected family contribution (EFC)
- Enrollment status (full-time or part-time and whether enrollment will be for the full academic year or less)
- Total cost of school attendance

Stafford Loans

Stafford Loans are offered by the government to students enrolled in American institutions of higher education. These loans are a good option because they usually charge lower interest than a private loan. Even better, subsidized Stafford Loans will pay interest during school and during deferment if you qualify. Unsubsidized Stafford Loans will not pay your interest, but they will still likely offer lower rates than most commercial loans.

Chapter Lessons

- Planning for school starts years in advance of attendance.
- Consider all options to pay for school.
- Apply for scholarships, grants, federal aid, and other loans.
- Most of all, save, save, save.
- The less you borrow, the less you'll have to worry about when you finish school.

13

Debt Reduction

What would a personal finance book be without a section on reducing personal debt? Debt is simply a fact of life and, while it's not all bad, too much of it can be a problem. Whether your debt could finance a small army or it's enough to keep you from buying your dream home, it's worth considering some options to find your way out of this seemingly bottomless pit. After all, too much debt can affect your personal and professional life.

In this chapter, we will cover two topics related to debt:

- How to destroy your financial and personal life through too much debt

- How to get your financial and personal life back after being buried in too much debt

How to Destroy Your Financial and Personal Life through Too Much Debt

You Can't Touch This

Why is it that celebrities who make more money than most of us end up buried in debt? Simple. They spend more than they earn. In my younger days, wearing pants with leg width to match the inseam was all the rage. Throw on a faux tux shirt with ruffled lapels and inflated sleeves and I could do no wrong. While I could dance a mean running man, I was far from a mega successful pop star. My inspiration, however, was one of the biggest stars on the planet.

MC Hammer, at the peak of his career, had a net worth of approximately $33 million. Twelve million dollars was spent to build his dream home in northern

California, which was later sold for $5.3 million. It was widely believed that Hammer once employed 200 people spending $6.8 million to cover their expenses.[1]

Sadly, Hammer (née Stanley Kirk Burrell) later went on to file bankruptcy. Financially speaking, Hammer's story is a cautionary tale. Sure, few of us will ever earn tens of millions of dollars, yet far too many of us find ourselves in a situation not unlike Hammer's: buried in debt and on the verge of bankruptcy.

How Does One Collapse under the Weight of Excessive Debt?

Spend more than you earn. Too easy. If you make X and you spend Y, guess what? As simple as this sounds, far too many people do just this. Often, they believe that the life-changing payout is just around the corner. A big raise. A lottery ticket. Something will work out. I'm all for having faith, but I'm entirely against it being blind.

Deplete your emergency fund. So, you're smart and live well within your means. Not good enough. Life is full of surprises and many of them can cause you to incur unforeseen expenses. These expenses can wipe you out.

Ignore your debt balances. Not knowing what you have prevents you from fixing the problem.

Ignore the government. Forgot to file your tax returns? Under-reported income? Settling up with the government can prove to be a costly surprise and one that will add to your existing debt load.

Ignore your health. Not taking care of yourself can prove costly. Getting sick can be the worst thing that happens to you, your family, and your finances. And not having health insurance can wipe you out. Stay healthy—eat well, sleep well, and exercise. And make sure you have health insurance.

How to Get Your Financial and Personal Life Back after Being Buried in Too Much Debt

Where there's a will, there's a way. If you're truly committed to working your way out of debt, there just might be some hope. With some hard work, discipline, and a little luck, you could find yourself debt free and living life again

---

[1] "The Talk of the Town: Under the Hammer." *The New Yorker*, August 26, 1996.

on your terms (not the bank's). Here is my program for working your way out of debt.

Understand the Problem

Sometimes getting to the underlying psychology is the most important step in the process. Why did you get to this point? Ever notice that some of the most successful people you know are drowning in debt? This isn't because they don't earn enough. It's because they live beyond their means. Spending money is fun and, when the supply of it is seemingly endless thanks to innumerable debt options, it's easy to indulge in consumer pursuits. Compounding matters is the fact that it often seems that everyone around us is doing the same thing. Borrowing to spend seems like the norm and we all want to be like everyone else, right? In the midst of this, it's hard to gauge the consequences. If friends and neighbors buy larger homes and nicer cars, shouldn't we do the same? Unfortunately, we have a tendency to focus on the success stories while ignoring the failures. People rarely talk about filing for bankruptcy or having their cars repossessed, but they love to tell you about their new houseboat. So, for starters, understand that just because everyone does it doesn't make it right. There is no such thing as a free lunch and the adage could not be more relevant than now, in the age of debt-fueled excess.

Accept the Problem

So, you understand that this is a problem. Borrowing to spend indiscriminately has consequences. What about you? If you've done this and you're running up a massive debt balance, you need to take ownership of your problem. I have known more than my fair share of people in this position and not one has stood up and said, "I screwed up. I took on more than I could ever afford." If you intend to fix the problem, first admit that you have one. While the next steps won't be easy, at least you'll be moving forward.

Analyze the Problem

Now the fun part. When did the problem start and where does it stand now? Did it begin with a gummy bear addiction in kindergarten? Borrowing from classmates to fuel this destructive habit? Running up dental bills and creating bad blood with the playground loan sharks? Did the gummy bears morph into designer clothes? Narcotics? Strippers? OK, if so, you might need a book other than this one to help solve your problems. Let's assume you're buried in debt and need to stop the bleeding. Figure out why you spend so much. Are you bored? Perhaps you need a hobby. Did you fail to read the fine print? Start reading.

Outline the Trouble Spots

Where did this mess begin? Was it overindulgence or just bad finance? The former is clearly a bigger problem than the latter because it indicates a major psychological challenge that you will need to overcome. Compulsive shoppers require serious reprogramming and, while I consider myself good at verbally beating people into submission, this is one area where I've fallen short (just ask any of my ex-girlfriends). However, once you've solved this problem, it's time to get to work.

Make a List of All Balances and Their Rates

Do you really know how much debt you have? It's easy to bury your head in the sand, but taking stock of everything you owe is essential to reducing your debt. What are your debt balances? Include credit cards, mortgages, auto loans, student loans, loan-shark loans, and so on. If you owe it, list it. Make sure you include the balances owed, monthly payments, and interest rate. These are all important and no one item is more important than the others.

Arrange your list from highest interest rate to lowest interest rate. Start by arranging the list from highest interest rate to lowest interest rate. The interest is the cost of financing so it's important to know how much you're ultimately being charged for each amount of outstanding debt.

Consolidate or refinance. Which items can you consolidate, renegotiate, or refinance? Getting these numbers down could help immensely.

Make a plan to start paying down higher-interest-rate debts. Now that you've got things down to a manageable level, it's time to start budgeting for the payments. You will need to understand what your monthly payments will be and how much you'll need to save from your after-tax income to cover these payments.

Increase your income. This is a tough one. You're probably working as hard as possible but, unfortunately, that just might not be good enough. Can you take on a second job working nights or weekends? You could also consider setting up a small business. If you have a particular set of skills, it may be easier than you think. Working more than you have to is not always fun, but neither is declaring bankruptcy.

Budget to save. Throughout this book, we discuss ways to save money, what to spend money on, and when to spend it. Review these pieces of advice carefully and apply what you save to paying down your debt.

Set goals and track accomplishments. This is the best part of all. Set realistic goals for yourself and make sure you're reaching them. Reward yourself when you achieve your goals. Nothing wrong with a nice dinner, a ballgame, or a trip to the racetrack (OK, just kidding) when you hit your goal. This will give you something to look forward to and make this whole process a heck of a lot of fun.

For many people, debt reduction can be one of the greatest challenges they'll face. It's not easy but, if you're truly focused on improving your situation, you can make it happen. And if all else fails, just marry rich.

Chapter Lessons

- Too much debt will affect your financial life as well as your personal life.

- Acknowledge the problem and work on paying down your debts.

- While it requires patience and determination, it will be well worth it when you find yourself debt free.

14

Investment Basics

One of the most important things you can learn in life is how to invest. It surprises me how many smart, talented people I've met over the years who excel professionally and personally, yet show no interest in learning this life-enhancing skill. As we've learned throughout this book, money is a fact of life. If you choose to ignore it, you may fall short of your life goals. We've spent time discussing why it's important to save your money, but what about the concept of growing it? One of the greatest clichés in the world is, "Your money should work for you." I couldn't agree more. Money creates opportunities for those who have it and those who use it. If you're the one who has it, then giving it to those who can use it creates an opportunity for everyone. When you deposit your hard-earned savings in the bank, you earn a rate of interest. That interest can accumulate, giving you the chance to spend income you otherwise would not have had. At the same time, the bank is able to take the money you deposited and lend it to others who need to buy a home or start a business. In the end, your funds create income for you and opportunity for others. Sure, this is an oversimplified and arguably overly optimistic look at investing, but the simple principle remains: Money should be put to work.

In this chapter, we discuss three topics:

- Investment basics
- Investment jargon
- Portfolio theory

Investment Basics

Consider the following example. Your friend just started a business and is looking for investors. His hope is to grow his business into a multimillion-dollar enterprise, and getting in on the ground floor could prove quite lucrative. With your investment, your friend has the seed capital to hire employees, purchase equipment, and pay for advertising. If his business grows, your stake is worth more. One day he sells his business and your little investment has paid off handsomely. His dream became a reality because of your investment while your retirement is secure.

Consider another example. Your favorite company just went public. You bought shares of the company and, because of investors like you, the company's stock price moves higher. The company sold its shares to investors in the initial public offering (IPO) so your purchasing the shares will benefit the person who sells them to you. Or will it? The company benefits as well from a rising share price. It can sell more shares to the public and raise more capital when it needs it. That's capital it can then deploy to develop and sell new, innovative products to loyal customers like you.

OK, enough Finance 101. The simple lesson here is that money creates opportunity. So, why do so many people ignore this simple principle? My friends and family members seem intimidated by it? The idea of investing can be daunting: What do I buy? What if I lose? Who do I trust? Part of the problem is a general lack of understanding given that investment concepts are rarely explained. We'll try to change that.

Don't Jump the Financial Shark

As a self-proclaimed tenured professor of pop culture (I teach at the University of Reuben Advani), I've focused my teaching pursuits on the Jump-the-Shark Theory. If you grew up watching *Happy Days* or at least caught glimpses of it in syndication, you know that the character Fonzi was a defining force in American culture. As a kid, I wanted to be the Fonz. His unsurpassed level of cool was inspirational. This came crashing down when one season, the show's brilliant writers decided to place this paradigm of timeless cool on a pair of water skis and send him jumping over a deadly shark off the coast of California. Even as a grade schooler with no concept of screen writing, I found this highly disturbing. To this day, I'm haunted by the imagery of a grown man in a leather jacket and swim trunks water skiing.

In Hollywood, when a TV show is on the verge a ratings meltdown, the writers have been known to "jump the shark," meaning they will throw some entirely incongruous storyline into the mix to shock and awe viewers. Rarely does this work because viewers know what they want. A show about a group of friends in 1950s Milwaukee should not send central characters to California to jump killer animals. The show would never be the same.

So, what does this have to do with personal finance? All too often, we find ourselves jumping the fiscal shark. You're working hard, collecting your payment and benefits, and, all of a sudden, a bank offers you the chance to own your dream home. Throw everything into this home and your life will magically improve. Jump the fiscal shark. A friend of mine became obsessed with self-improvement seminars and, as her financial situation continued to deteriorate, she spent more and more on these seminars seeking guidance. This culminated in her writing a check for several thousand dollars to pay for a master program. The sales rep told her, "Think of this as an investment in your future." To this day, she still lives each day on the verge of financial collapse.

Fonzi never should have jumped the shark and neither should you. There is nothing wrong with being a risk taker, but being smart about the risks you take will help you get the most out of life. A calculated risk is smart. A blind one is not.

Investment Jargon

Rate of Return

One of the most important concepts in all of finance, the rate of return on an investment lets you know how much you've earned compared to what you invested. Suppose you invested $1,000 and next year your account has $1,100; you would have earned ten percent. Simple enough, right? Rates of return become more complex when measured over an extended period of time, a topic covered in more detail in many finance books. For our purposes, we'll just focus on simple returns and what to use them for. First, understanding how much your portfolio earns allows you to understand its performance. To state that your portfolio made money isn't of much help. A one-percent rate of return will prove far less beneficial than a ten-percent rate of return. In terms of your lifestyle and life goals, you need to make sure your rate of return keeps pace with your financial goals.

Required Rate of Return

Suppose your financial guru tells you that you will need to earn eight percent annually to achieve your goal of retiring at age 55. You need to ensure that you are achieving this target. Having this goal will force you to seek out investment opportunities or investment advisers who can deliver these results. And if your returns consistently fall below this rate, it's time to make some changes.

Present Value

Like rate of return, present value is a biggie in the financial universe. Present value is the idea that a dollar received tomorrow has a lower value than a dollar received today. The formula for this can be a little confusing for you poets out there but, in case you're curious, here goes:

$$PV=FV/(1+r)^n$$

The PV in the equation represents the value of a payment in the future valued today. FV represents the payment made in the future. In the denominator, we add one to r (which represents the rate of return, or more precisely, the rate per period of time). The rate of return theoretically represents the risk level associated with the future payments. The higher the risk, the higher the rate of return. And finally, the denominator is raised to the nth power. N represents the number of periods that the rate of return is based on. If FV is paid three years in the future and the rate of return is based on years, n would be three. There you have it, an entire year's worth of MBA finance in a few sentences. If you're interested in learning more about this, might I recommend the perennial classic—*The Wall Street MBA*? For our purposes, understand that this formula is used in more areas of finance than we have space to elaborate on.

Leverage

Leverage is the idea that you can borrow against your invested funds to magnify the impact of your investment dollars. For example, if you borrow three dollars for every one dollar you invested, you have a three-to-one leverage ratio. Suppose the investment doubles. The four dollars you started with is now eight dollars. After paying back the three you started with, you're left with five dollars. Even though you ponied up one dollar of your own money, you earned an additional four dollars by investing borrowed funds. All in all, you made a sizable return. Get the idea? Leverage works great in boom times. It doesn't work so well in a bust. If your investment value drops, you're still on the hook for what you borrowed. Before long, you're struggling to raise capital to cover losses on borrowed funds. Not a pleasant situation. Just ask anyone who used to work for Lehman Brothers.

Compounding Interest

Interest starts to earn interest on itself—one of the greatest concepts in finance. In other words, your money grows because your interest payments are invested along with your principal. Before long, a small investment has grown into a fortune.

Rule of 72

If you frequent *Star Trek* conventions or have never been kissed, you might be able to explain the Rule of 72. Since neither applies to me, I'll stick with the basics. By dividing your annual rate of return or interest into 72, you can determine how long it takes for your money to double. For example, if your annual rate of return is 12 percent, it would take six years to double your money (72 divided by 12 is 6). Pretty neat.

Diversification

One of the most important and often overlooked lessons in investing is diversification. At the risk of oversimplifying things, the basic lesson here is to invest a little bit in everything: stocks, bonds, commodities, real estate, currency, and so on. Here's why. Markets go up and markets go down. That will never change. To insulate yourself from major market swings, it pays to diversify across asset classes. This way, if your stocks are down, perhaps your gold is up. This allows you to maintain steady returns and avoid catastrophic losses. True, there are always stories of people who put their life savings in Apple when it was $10 per share. But for every story like that, there are ten others about people who put their life savings in Enron when it was $70 per share. Stocks and markets go up and down and trying to predict which areas to invest in can make your head spin.

Portfolio Theory

When I took my first portfolio theory course in college, it left me utterly confused. I was haunted by images of Greek letters and statistical modeling that had me all but convinced that my only career options would be limited to shepherding or cult discipleship. A funny thing happened, however. The New York City dating scene taught me an important lesson that helped instill in me a love for finance. One night after work, a colleague of mine introduced me to the idea of portfolio theory. Out at a club, he approached a tall blond and managed to score her number. Later that evening, he struck up a conversation with a voluptuous brunette and managed to set up a date for the next day. A few more attractive ladies surfaced and, by the end of the night, he had five dates lined up. I asked him, "Why do you need so many dates?" "Portfolio Theory," he responded. "Markets go up and down. Markets are volatile. A diversified portfolio enables you to maintain steady returns and hedge against sector-based disruptions. So, if the blond becomes too needy, I spend more time with the brunette. If the brunette turns psycho, I go out with the redhead. Get the point." I got it. Unfortunately, my friend is still single.

Chapter Lessons

- It is important to brush up on financial basics in order to make sound financial decisions.

- Learning to speak the language of finance will help you maneuver a complex financial world.

- Understanding principles of portfolio management will help you survive and profit from market shifts.

15

Stock Market Investing

Growing up, my dad used to say he would never invest in stocks because the stock market is not for the average investor. He intimated that the market was rigged and, as I grew older, I began to wonder whether he just might be right. At the same time, I felt that he very well could be ignoring an investment opportunity of a lifetime as the stock market seemed to reach all-time highs on a regular basis. After careful analysis, I decided to recommend a stock pick to my dad so I presented him with the case for Coca-Cola. My friends would drink copious amounts of Coke, and the company had recently announced a discontinuation of its original formula only to have it reinstated after a brief period of time. All in all, this created a publicity coup for Coke, launched the Cola Wars, and shot the price of Coke stock through the roof. I begged my dad to buy shares of Coke, but he refused. Coke went on to become one of the most successful companies in history (with a stock price to match) and my dad kept out of the stock market settling for safer, low-yielding investments. Years have passed and I have studied the vagaries of the stock market. I can appreciate my dad's words of wisdom, but not without some revision. True, the stock market is not for the misinformed or ignorant. But, at the same time, it can be an effective way to recognize solid investment returns over the long run. But buyer, beware! The stock market is not for the novice investor. Do your own research and you just might find yourself generating steady returns.

Generations ago, buying stock in companies was something only the rich could afford to do. Thanks in part to technology, information can be shared faster and transaction costs can be less. What this means for the average person is that stock ownership is simply a fact of life in the twenty-first century. While it's important to consider investing in stocks, especially if you hope to achieve any level of financial independence, it's not good to invest in them if you don't understand them.

In this chapter, we will discuss several issues related to the stock market:

- How to analyze companies
- Stock market valuation
- What moves stock prices
- Smart investing
- Stock market funds

How to Analyze Companies

Earnings per share (EPS). This little number that appears at the very bottom of a company's income statement can be a key driver of its stock price. In essence, this number tells you how much a company earned during the last quarter or last year. Think of it in the following way: A company records everything it sold, subtracts everything it spent, and the difference is its net earnings. To simplify things for shareholders, this number is divided by the total number of outstanding shares, which gives you earnings per share. It's easier to understand this number as you can compare it to what you would pay for one share of stock. Wall Street banks and research firms study this number intensely and try to predict what this number will be in next reporting cycle. If the number that the company reports ends up being higher than what the Wall Street firms predicted, chances are the stock price will move higher. And, of course, if the number is lower than what the firms predicted, look out below.

Guidance. While the reported results are important, what management predicts can be even more important. The guidance that follows most every earnings report is crucial to determining the direction the company takes. Investors and analysts need to hear this from the horse's mouth so if guidance is strong, chances are the stock will move higher. Of course, if management guides higher and the next quarter misses, the stock will likely drop … along with the CEO's pay package.

Cash. It's nice to see cash on a company's balance sheet. And the more cash, the better, right? Not necessarily. Having too much cash can make investors nervous. It signals to the investment community that perhaps the company isn't doing enough to grow the company by hoarding so much cash. At the same time, a company that produces strong and steady cash flow can survive nearly any tough situation. So, what's better? Too much or too little cash? I'm going with too much. You can always spend cash, but making it is a different story. Look for companies with decent cash-generating abilities and decent cash reserves. How much is decent depends on the industry but, ideally, the company ranks among the best.

Debt. Generally speaking, less debt is better. As we've discovered, not all debt is bad, but companies with less debt are beholden to few and have greater financial flexibility. Stick with companies that have lower debt levels.

Growth. Ideally, a company should reveal signs of growth. Investors pay hefty premiums when buying stock for this elusive quality. And, likewise, when growth slows, these same investors can be merciless. In essence, when buying a share of stock, you're not only buying the company's performance today but also its expected performance in the future. When that performance shows signs of abating, you're less willing to pay as much. A team that signs a marquee player to a lucrative long-term contract recognizes that perhaps that player won't deliver a championship in the first few seasons but, longer term, that's the expectation. More importantly, the player needs to improve year after year. And if that player fails to show improvement or, worse, gets hurt, that player will be traded. Game over.

Dividends. The jury is out on this one. Companies pay dividends to their shareholders from time to time. These are generally cash payments although sometimes they're paid in stock. Some investors prefer to invest in companies that pay dividends as they can provide a source of income or, at the least, cash to invest elsewhere. Other investors avoid dividend-paying stocks as they believe their companies produce little to no growth. If they did, the dividend funds would be reinvested back into the company to capitalize on lucrative growth opportunities. Who's right? Depends who you ask. I recommend keeping a mix of dividend- and non-dividend-paying stocks in a portfolio.

Stock Market Valuation

How do you value a share of stock? This is the trillion-dollar question. Theories abound on how to value stocks, but the reality is if someone produced something consistently worthwhile, we'd all be rich. Nonetheless, analysts and investors make millions off of certain stock-pricing models, which include the following:

Dividend growth model. This nifty model is predicated on the idea that a stock is worth the present value of its future dividend payments. The math can be a bit complex, but the principle is basic. The stock is worth what it pays out into perpetuity. Here's the problem: Dividends are not always paid and, when they are, they may not reflect the true performance of a company.

Discounted cash flow model. This model makes an already complicated matter even more complex. The company is valued in its entirety based on the present value of future discounted cash flow. The sum of these present values produces the value of the company. This value can be divided by the total shares of outstanding stock to calculate the fair value of one share of stock.

Comparable multiples. This is probably the easiest and most practical means of calculating the value of a share of stock. An industry average price-to-earnings multiple is calculated. This number is multiplied by the expected earnings per share for the company to come up with its target share price.

What Moves Stock Prices

Several factors influence stock price movements in the short run.

Company changes. First and foremost, company changes, such as new-product launches, new market initiatives, changes in management, or internal restructuring, can move a company's stock price. Sometimes it can move higher and sometimes it can move lower, depending on how the news is perceived.

Earnings. Each quarter, analysts and investors eagerly await a company's earnings announcement like children on Christmas morning. The earnings number can be measured in many forms but it's usually some assessment of the company's profit. Analysts and investors study this number to determine whether it was better than expected, worse than expected, or in line with expectations. The better the number, the stronger the company's performance and, in turn, the greater the company value.

Insider buying. Insider buying of shares signals to the investor public that someone who is actively involved with the company has full confidence in the company's future prospects. This is a significant vote of confidence and can send the stock price higher.

Mergers and acquisitions. This news could cause the stock to move either way. In the past, a company making a bid on a target company would see its stock price drop given the liability and risk it might assume in the deal. Meanwhile, the target's price would increase given the assumed premium paid for it. Nowadays, that may not be the case. Oftentimes, a company will announce a proposed deal to gauge the investor public's reaction. If the reaction is favorable, the deal is more likely to move forward.

Analyst recommendations. These folks can make or break a company's stock price. Wall Street analysts carry a good deal of weight in the world of stock picking. An upgrade can send a company stock price soaring and a downgrade can send it crashing.

Stock splits. There is no rational explanation as to why a company stock will move after the announcement of a split. When a company's stock is split, there is no material change to the overall company value. However, investor perception may change simply based on the exchange to a higher number of shares, which lowers the stock price. In other words, receiving two shares for every one share can make a company seem more attractive to smaller investors. This could lead to increasing demand and a short-lived bump in price.

Economic news. The most complex of all variables to affect stock prices is economic news. GDP numbers, job numbers, inflation numbers, and any other regulatory change can affect a company's stock price. It's not entirely clear how any macroeconomic variable could affect a stock's price, but you can bet that major changes can prompt a move one way or the other.

Smart Investing

Building a Portfolio

Build a diversified portfolio of stocks but *never* keep all your money in the stock market. Here's why. The stock market is moody. Any number of events can trigger a stock market sell-off. Can a revolution in Equatorial Guinea trigger a sell off? It could. Does it mean that consumers buy fewer computers? Probably not, but if stock market indices fall, you can bet that computer stocks will fall as well. In other words, when the sky is falling, you better grab that umbrella. That umbrella is cash.

Consider what happened in 2008. At the onset of the financial crisis, banks were deemed insolvent and the entire financial services sector sold off. Meanwhile, companies like Apple sold off as well as investors believed that no one would own stocks for a very long time. As the dust settled, investors noticed something peculiar. People were buying technology in spite of painful economic conditions. And companies like Apple posted record numbers. As more people noticed this, Apple's stock started to rise. It became one of the best performing stocks in history and, within a few years, the most valuable company in the world.

The Existentialist Investor

Back when I considered myself semiliterate, I was struck by the teachings of the great existentialist philosophers. Sartre and Camus focused much of their writings on absurdity, which ultimately postulates that bad things happen to good people and good things happen to bad people. In other words, this runs against the grain of karmic beliefs in which case you create your own moral existence. So, what does any of this have to do with personal finance? Well, the stock market is absurd. I've spent decades trying to figure this one out, and that's my ultimate conclusion. Where's my Nobel Prize? Just because I espouse this view doesn't mean I will stop investing, however. It's because of this belief that I can be a better investor. In other words, you can research all you want, study your technical charts and balance sheets, and in the end your investment still goes sour. If you accept this risk, you too can thrive as a stock market investor.

What Goes Up, Must Come Down

Is it possible for a stock to go up forever? Sure. Is it likely? No. For a stock to continue to climb higher, growth must be sustained. In other words, the company must continue to sell more products and services year after year. Eventually, markets become saturated or competitors take an aggressive stand and chip away at a company's market share. In spite of this, many of us will buy a company's stock and never sell. This is absurd. Unless you believe a company will grow infinitely, there is little justification for this. Of course, there are companies that reach all-time stock price highs every few years, but that doesn't necessarily mean that these stocks are necessarily good investments. Consider a stock that hits an all-time high every ten years or so. That all-time high could only be a few points higher than the last one, yet you waited a full decade for. In that case, what you earned over the course of the decade is probably less than what you would have earned in a simple savings account. So, the moral to this story is this: Don't be afraid to sell a winning stock. No one ever lost money taking a profit. Sure, you might leave some money on the table, but I for one would rather take profits too soon than losses too late. Many experts advise selling a small portion of your position each time a stock hits an all-time high.

Stock Market Funds

How do you get rich trading stocks? You don't. It is nearly impossible for the average investor to make serious money in the stock market. Sure, you can get lucky and invest all your money in the start-up that just invented the smartphone that does laundry but, realistically, you wouldn't place all your eggs in one basket. More likely, you'll invest in several companies across several industries. Some will go up and some will go down. At the end of the year, assuming you've done your homework and made wise choices, you might fare slightly better than the overall stock market. Was it worth it? Depends. If you enjoyed the time you spent researching the stocks and making these decisions, perhaps. More importantly, if the amount of money you made above and beyond what you would have made investing in the overall stock market compensates you adequately for your time, then sure, smart move. So, who gets rich in the stock market? Fund managers. Not only do they collect a management fee for investing your hard-earned dollars but, in some cases, they also take a hefty percentage of any gains their fund produces. Fair or not, this is the way the system works.

Funds can offer the ever-so-important benefit of diversification. Sure, you can put all your money in one company, but don't come crying to me when the CEO skips town as a result of an accounting scandal. At that point, you will be wishing you had invested in a fund. At least you won't lose everything. If you had invested in a sector-based fund targeting the banking sector, you would have likely seen a serious drop in value as the entire industry was pummeled by the credit crisis. Just as you should never put all your money into any one stock, you shouldn't put it into any one sector-based fund.

Investing in a fund can be the easiest way to invest in the financial markets without having to worry about it. Think of fund investments as a neat way to have someone else manage your financial affairs without paying too much for their services. Of course, the downside of this is that someone else is managing your financial affairs. So, do your homework and find your own stocks to invest in or invest your money with a fund.

Mutual Funds

Mutual funds are massive pools of investment dollars designed to offer you a chance to invest in a class of securities or particular industry. These funds are usually managed by a team of professionals who spend days and nights pouring through data, speaking to company managers, and analyzing market trends. Like sports stars, many of them are ranked and their pay is largely tied to performance. Needless to say, a bad fund manager usually has a short shelf life. In addition to doing all of your dirty work, the funds usually charge one percent or less. No-load funds can even prove more compelling as they do not charge commissions on transactions. Loads are commissions paid to brokers involved with selling mutual funds. These fees can range from three percent to more than eight percent. Ultimately, this eats into your returns.

ETFs

ETFs are one of the best things to happen to the financial world since the calculator was invented. An ETF (exchange traded fund) is a simple portfolio composed of several companies within an industry and trades under its own ticker symbol. Buying an ETF allows you to basically buy an entire industry. This way, you are protected against company risk. Should one company underperform for any reason, chances are another will pick up any resulting shortfall in business. While you're unlikely to see any astronomical gains as if you invested in one stellar company, you're hedged against major risks. And, best of all, you need not worry about researching each and every company. ETFs have fees, but they are substantially lower than those of mutual funds.

Hedge Funds

The funny thing about hedge funds is that they really don't hedge much of anything. In the early days of hedge-fund investing, fund managers would adopt strategies geared at preserving capital while maximizing returns. In those days, the idea was to create an investment pool for sophisticated investors. A savvy manager would manage the fund in such a way that positions would be properly hedged avoiding catastrophic losses. Oh, how the times have changed. More recently, fund managers seem focused on maximizing returns through excessive leverage. Should a fund manager blow up one fund, no problem. There's always another one ready to start.

Hedge funds are now pools with minimal disclosure requirements, managed by individuals and groups who are highly incentivized to take on as much risk as possible. So much for hedging. A hedge fund can invest in just about anything and, as long as returns are strong, investors ask few questions. Most hedge funds will require you to pony up a substantial amount, so it's certainly not the best choice for the average investor.

Chapter Lessons

- Stock analysis can be based on several interacting factors.
- Stock valuation is derived from sophisticated financial models that are often highly speculative.
- Smart investing requires an understanding of market behavior.
- Stock market funds can provide a low-stress way to invest in the market.

16

Bond Market Investing

Remember the days when your grandmother would give you a 20-dollar savings bond for your birthday? If you waited 30 years, you could cash it in for the full 20-dollar value. Meanwhile, you spent $10 per year to store it securely in a bank locker. Things have certainly changed over the years. Nowadays, bond investing is becoming an integral part of building wealth. In this chapter, we'll cover three topics:

- Bond basics
- Bond types
- Bond market

Bond Basics

Bond Prices and Interest Rates

OK, this might be one of the most challenging areas of finance to explain, but I'll do my best. Bond prices tend to move in the opposite direction of interest rates. If you hold your bond until it matures, this should not matter to you. But suppose you buy a bond that pays five percent interest. If interest rates creep higher, your bond is worth less. An investor would rather buy a newly issued bond of comparable risk that pays a higher rate than own your bond, which was issued at a lower rate. In other words, your bond is less attractive given that its interest is relatively lower than a comparable new issue. Similarly, if interest rates drop, your bond suddenly seems more attractive given its higher rate and, therefore, should appreciate in price. There you have it. You're now ready for a job at the Fed.

Bond Features

Issue amount. This is the amount expected to be raised by the bond offering.

Principal. This is the nominal amount or the amount on which the issuer pays interest. Often known as par value or face value, bonds are denominated relative to face value, which is the amount you would receive when the bond matures. If face value is $1,000, then that is the amount you would receive if you held the bond to maturity.

Maturity. Bonds have a maturity date or date upon which the issuer pays back the principal (face or par value). This can be short-term, which is typically one to five years; medium-term, which is six to twelve years; or long-term, which is greater than twelve years.

Interest or coupon. This is the payment you receive semiannually or annually and is typically a fixed percentage of face value. Some bonds will offer interest that floats against some interest rate index such as LIBOR (London Interbank Offer Rate). A five-percent coupon bond with a $1,000 face value means the bond will pay five dollars in interest each year. In other words, you receive five dollars payment each year.

Price. Bonds, like most investments, will fluctuate in price. While a bond will have its face value, its purchase price could be higher or lower than its face value. This is important because it will affect your rate of return. For example, if you pay more than the face value for a bond, your rate of return will be less than your simple interest rate. In other words, you lose a bit of money on the bond purchase assuming you hold it to maturity. The interest payments, however, offset these losses.

Credit quality. Perhaps one of the most important attributes of a bond is its credit quality. Determined by the credit-rating agencies, this gives investors an idea as to how secure the issue is. The higher the rating, the less likely the company is to default. The lower the rating, the higher the likelihood of default. Riskier bonds, in theory, should earn a higher yield.

Yield. Here's where it gets interesting. The yield covers the return you earn on a bond based on the price you paid. If you paid a steep discount to face value, chances are your yield will be pretty high. For example, you paid $800 for a bond that has a five-percent coupon. Your simple yield would be the $50 you earn each year divided by the $800 you paid for the bond, or 6.25 percent. Yield can take on more complex forms including the granddaddy of all, which is yield to maturity. Entire books have been written about the mathematical complexities of yield to maturity, so I won't bore you with the details. Just know that this measurement is the most credible assessment of what your bond earns while factoring in time value of money.

Call provision. A company may retain the right to repay the debt prior to maturity, meaning it can call the bond or buy it back. The call price usually offers a premium above the current price, offering investors a premium for having to sell their bond back.

Bond Types

Government, municipal, corporate—it's enough to make your head spin! While some may be more secure than others, keep in mind that the more secure, the lower the yield. Or, as discussed earlier, lower risk, lower reward. Government bonds, especially U.S. Treasuries, tend to be the safest investments in the world. As such, don't expect to pay for that jet using the interest payments you receive from holding one. People buy treasuries for safety and stability. Think of treasuries as the date to the prom who has good manners, shows up on time, and will engage in candid small talk over the course of the evening. Low-grade corporate is the date that shows up late, gets drunk, and dances on the table. High risk and at times unsettling, but can often lead to a memorable evening. So, what's right for you? Depends. Generally, the older you get, the less risk you will want to assume. After all, wipe out your retirement savings speculating on junk bonds at the age of 80 and you may have difficulty recovering. For even younger investors, similar lessons hold. Never put all of your eggs in one basket. Speculating is fine, but make sure you're only placing a small amount of your overall portfolio in any one investment.

Government Bonds

Typically, government bonds pay very low interest but are probably the safest thing you can own. They are considered to be risk free, given that the U.S. government has never defaulted on its debt (not yet, at least). Buy these if you need security and stable returns. Keep in mind that sometimes your returns on U.S. Treasuries will barely keep pace with the rate of inflation. In fact, you could see your purchasing power diminish if inflation is on the rise.

Municipal Bonds

Issued by municipalities as the name implies, municipal bonds are often related to the financing of a public works project. A stadium, a hydroelectric dam, a highway—these are all projects that might involve muni bond funding. The advantages of muni bonds can be a federal tax exemption. That's right—the interest you earn on muni bonds can be free of federal taxes, meaning more money in your pocket! Keep in mind that rates on these bonds may be relatively lower than other investments of similar risk. If you're lucky enough to fall into a high-tax bracket, muni bonds might be just what you need.

Corporate Bonds

Riskiest of all, these bonds are issued by corporations in an effort to raise capital. They can be stable and secure when issued by solid companies with strong financials to match and volatile and risky when issued by companies with relatively weak financials. And, of course, your returns should match this. The highest-yielding bonds are often referred to as "junk," meaning their issuers tend to be weak and carry a higher probability of default than their more secure corporate counterparts. What this means for you is higher risk and the possibility of a higher reward. No guarantees here but, if you buy a junk bond and the company survives, you could profit handsomely. On the other hand, the company collapses and you could lose most if not all of your investment. Do not mess with junk bonds unless you are well versed in this area of finance and, even then, only invest a small portion of your nest egg.

Bond Market

Buying bonds on your own is something you should probably avoid unless you really know what you're doing. The bond market is a complex labyrinth controlled by a relatively small consortium of bond market insiders. Think overweight, cigar-chomping, suspender-wearing alpha males. OK, maybe I'm exaggerating a bit. They don't all wear suspenders. The bottom line is that without the right know-how and contacts within the investment world, you run the risk of paying too much for a bond. Should you insist on going down this road, here are two things you should be aware of—the primary market and the secondary market.

Primary bond market. When corporations issue bonds directly to the public, this issuance takes place in the primary market. Investment bankers, lawyers, accountants, and corporate executives work to price the offering and everyone who buys into the offering pays the same price for the bond. Getting in on the offering requires good contacts and can sometimes prove pretty difficult. Not to worry. You can always turn to the secondary market.

Secondary market. Once a bond is issued, it can usually be bought or sold in the secondary market. Unlike many stocks that trade on exchanges in the secondary market, bonds are generally traded over the counter, meaning they are based on negotiated sales between buyers and sellers by way of proprietary trading systems. Translation: You can get badly hurt on pricing. Be very careful buying bonds in the secondary market. I'll be the first to tell you this. My first experience buying a bond in this market did not work out so well. Being a Wall Street legend in my own mind, I decided to throw my hat into the bond-trading ring. I found a lovely Brazilian industrial company that listed some medium-grade corporate bonds. I logged into my online brokerage account and, eager to officially solidify my status as a bond trader, I placed a market order. The bond was set to mature in six months and both the interest and yield seemed strong. I sat back and savored my financial achievement. The following year, when reviewing my annual summary, I noticed something odd. My bond interest was far lower than expected and I showed a net loss on the bond. This had to be a mistake. I called my online broker's help line and spoke to a rep who assured me that we would get to the bottom of this mess. Within a matter of seconds, he responded that the numbers were correct. Furthermore, he highlighted the fact that, overall, my return on this purchase was negative! Negative! As if I held the bond to maturity I would still lose money. Or, to think of it another way, I loaned the company money and paid them a few extra bucks for that privilege. So, what went wrong, you ask? Basically, I paid a hefty premium when purchasing the bond. Given that I placed a market order, I did not stipulate any pricing parameters. The broker executed the trade at the highest possible price at the time. And the interest payment that I thought I was receiving had already been paid. I bought the bond the day after the second to last coupon payment was made. In other words, I was an idiot. Lesson learned. Leave bond trading to bond experts. If you want to invest in bonds, which I strongly encourage you to do, make sure you do your homework and buy into a low-fee bond mutual fund or bond ETF.

Chapter Lessons

- Bonds are difficult to buy and sell so make sure you do your homework.

- Ideally, purchase bonds in the primary market.

- Make sure you study the bonds credit quality and yield when deciding on whether to buy it.

- The easiest way to benefit from bonds in a portfolio is through a low-fee bond mutual fund or ETF.

17

Real Estate Investing

Investing in real estate can be intimidating. It's not something I advise everyone to do but, for a select few, it can offer a good investment opportunity and can build wealth over a lifetime. To determine if real estate investing makes sense for you, ask yourself the following questions:

1. Do I enjoy playing Monopoly?

2. Do I have a picture of Donald Trump next to my bed?

3. Do I enjoy monitoring interest rates?

4. Do I enjoy building spreadsheets?

If you answered yes to one or more of these questions, real estate investing might make sense for you. We all have a crazy uncle or arm's-length friend who wants to rope us in to some hair-brained real estate deal. And most of us have learned that if it sounds too good to be true, it probably is. Yet real estate investing doesn't have to be all bad and, in fact, it can be pretty darn good. The basic principle in real estate investing is to ensure that your rate of return exceeds your cost of borrowing.

In this chapter, we'll cover these two topics:

• Real estate basics

• Property management

Real Estate Basics

How Real Estate Investing Works

The simple premise behind income-generating properties is this: Your rate of return must exceed your cost of capital. If you earn ten percent returns and your cost of capital is five percent, you've made money! Of course, there's more to the equation than just this. Investors will also look for capital appreciation, meaning they'll hope the property value appreciates over time and, assuming they sell it, they will recognize some healthy gains. That should boost overall returns in excess of financing costs. And yet another advantage is depreciation. The assessed depreciation on a property is tax deductible, which can offset income gains on the property.

When looking at properties to buy, consider the following:

Low maintenance. This is very important. Do your homework and make sure you're not buying a money pit.

Good price. As the old saying goes, "You make your money on the buy." In other words, the lower price you get, the more you make when you sell. Profound. Shocking how many people lose sight of this when buying an investment property, however.

Favorable bank financing. If you can't achieve the most favorable lending terms, a dream deal can become a nightmare.

Value appreciation. Learn as much as you can about the neighborhood to determine whether property values will increase. Are they building a Starbucks around the corner? That could be a very good sign. Are they selling guns next door? Probably not such a good sign.

Advantages

The obvious advantage of real estate investing is the ability to create strong returns. Because so much of real estate is dependent upon leverage, one can build wealth quickly and effectively through real estate investing. But beware— this is a high-stakes game and one wrong move and that wealth can soon turn into massive debt. At the same time, the tax benefits can prove compelling. Specifically, the depreciation on a property can offset some of your tax liability. When you buy a property, like any other asset, the property loses value over time. This allows you to deduct the estimated depreciation against your income, which can reduce your tax liability at the end of the year. For investors with healthy income, this can be an effective strategy to reduce an otherwise hefty tax burden.

Disadvantages

Where to begin? For starters, real estate investing requires a colossal amount of paperwork. Appraisals, spreadsheets, loan documents, and so on! If you think your office is cluttered now, you ain't seen nothing yet. Additionally, dealing with banks can be painstakingly tedious and very frustrating. Just when you think your financing is approved, the lender can pull it or request more information. But the biggest disadvantage associated with real estate investing is simply this: You can lose a ton of money. Just as some of the largest fortunes in history have been made in this area, some of the largest fortunes have been lost as well. We all hear about the success stories, but we rarely hear about the failures. Because so much of your investment is dependent on factors beyond your control, such as interest rates, property values, and natural disasters, you can see your fortunes dissolve overnight. Good real estate investors have a tolerance for risk, strong negotiation skills, and good business instincts. If you don't fit this profile, stay away.

Don't Get Flipped Off

One of the fastest ways to make money in real estate is also one of the fastest ways to lose your shirt. If you're a cable TV watcher, you've probably channel-surfed your way into more than one show about buying and selling property. The folks that do this are known as property flippers, and they generally look for cheap properties that they can rehab and sell quickly. While this practice is often frowned upon by real estate professionals, the fact is that any opportunity is fair game in a free enterprise world. So, if flipping properties is your thing, go for it. Just be careful. Here's why. All too often, flippers jump on properties in haste and fail to give sufficient thought to renovation costs and desirability of the location. Once over budget and facing little rental interest, flippers can even sell for less than what they paid, causing them to incur huge losses. Beware of these risks if you decide to become a property flipper.

Types of Real Estate Investments

There are two ways to make money in real estate. The first is capital appreciation. Buy something today, sell it for more tomorrow, and you've made money. This requires patience, and you must make sure that your costs of maintaining the property as well as any other costs do not eat into your overall gains. The other way to make money is through income. Buy a property, rent it out, and the rental income you generate each month will hopefully exceed all of your monthly expenses. This can be a nice income supplement, and an added benefit can be any gains you recognize if and when you sell your property. Rarely does this type of thing happen overnight but, for the patient investor, this can be the slow and steady approach to winning the wealth game.

Property Management

You can hire someone to manage your property, but that person will undoubtedly take a hefty share of your profits. A property manager can charge between seven and ten percent of your monthly gross income. After you subtract other costs and expenses from monthly rent, you may not be left with much. It pays to do it yourself and, while it can be a pain at times, the money you save can make it worthwhile. It also gives you the ability to take control of your investment and manage it as efficiently as possible. This can spell happier tenants and fatter profits. A good situation for everyone involved. In order to manage your property effectively, make sure you do the following:

Track all tenants. Keep a list of their contact information (name, address, phone, e-mail) as well as specifics of their lease terms (start date, end date) handy. You should keep this on your computer as well as on your phone. If you're on the road, you may need to respond to their requests and having this information available will be helpful.

List all utility bills. Make sure you have a list of all bills you pay on the property each month and when they are due.

Keep track of all bank statements. Stay on top of all mortgage statements and bank deposits. Ideally, opt for electronic delivery of these statements.

Set up auto pay online. Recurring payments should be made through an online banking set up.

List all service providers. Make sure you have a numbers for plumbers, roofers, handymen, electricians, locksmiths, and carpenters available at all times. If possible, get to know one of each type of professional and let them know that you may be forwarding them repair requests from your tenants directly. This will streamline things and save you time and money.

Chapter Lessons

- Real estate can be an effective way to supplement your income and build wealth.

- Understand the risks and hassles associated with real estate investing before you decide to pursue it.

- Just as fortunes can be made in real estate, fortunes can be lost.

18

Playing It Safe

For many people, sleeping well at night is far more important than wealth building. Sure, taking on risk may increase your chances of growing your money, but it is not for the faint of heart. For those of you who prefer to stash your savings under the mattress, I suggest you consider ways to keep what you have safe and manage potential risk. This approach won't land you on the cover of *Forbes*, but it may bring you peace of mind. And, even if you're a financial gun-slinging maverick in the early stages of your career, it makes sense to play it safe at times. I'll leave it to you and the investment gurus to determine when you should protect yourself and how much protection you need. In this chapter, we'll consider these issues:

- Bank accounts
- Certificates of deposit
- Money market accounts
- Protecting yourself with insurance

Bank Accounts

Clearly having a bank account is a must for everyone.

Checking Account

Basic checking. To keep things simple, a basic checking account allows you to deposit your money in the bank, access it when you need to, and earn interest in the process. This allows you to pay your bills by check or withdraw cash from an automated teller machine (ATM). The interest you earn can be meager and the ATM will likely charge you each time you make a withdrawal. Nonetheless, a basic checking account is usually a must for most people given its low balance requirements and easy access to funds. Just make certain that you are not assuming unnecessary fees or you'll find that you are supporting the bank more than you are supporting yourself.

Free checking. The great thing about a free checking account is that it can offer you unlimited check writing and no maintenance fees. More importantly, it may not even require a minimum balance. Theoretically, you could keep five dollars in your account and write checks for twenty-five cents. In fact, a friend of mine did just that. He was so disgusted with his alma mater that he used to write a check for pennies each year during the annual fundraising campaign. The school was under obligation to deposit every check, and he realized that they spent more on postage and administrative costs than the amount of his check. By the way, I don't recommend you do this. Theoretically, however, it is possible with a free checking account.

Express. For the tech savvy, this account requires you to bank by phone, ATM, or computer. If you should desire human contact, expect to pay fees when you use a teller. People on the go find this type of account particularly useful.

Interest bearing. The interest-bearing checking account will require a minimum deposit to open the account, a minimum balance maintained, and will charge monthly fees if you don't maintain the minimum balance. The interest is nominal and restrictions can be severe. I suggest avoiding this type of account as it is easy to dip below the minimum balance requirement.

What to compare when shopping around for the best checking account:

- Interest rates
- Minimum balances
- Monthly fees
- Transaction fees
- Check-writing limits
- Overdraft fees

Savings Accounts

Clearly better than most checking accounts when it comes to earning interest, this is a good way to keep your money safe while it grows, albeit slowly, over time. The problem, however, is getting your money out, which will likely require a trip to the bank or, in some cases, the ATM.

ATM Fees

ATM fees are the greatest thing to happen to the banking industry since Mr. Potter took over the bank in Bedford Falls. Every time you need money, the bank gets paid, and these fees can all add up. A typical ATM can charge $2 per withdrawal or more. And if you're like many people who no longer like to carry too much cash, this means a stop at the ATM each time you need cash. Pit stops like these can mean tens of dollars each month just in withdrawal fees. Consider this: You maintain an average balance of $1,000 in your account. Each month, you make eight ATM withdrawals with each one costing $2.50. That's $20 per month, or $240 per year! Your account only earns one percent interest! Within a few years, you will have depleted your entire account in ATM fees alone. So, what can you do when the bank holds your money and you need it? Cash back. If you use your bank card as a debit card, you can ask for cash back on purchases. Let's say you spend $50 on groceries. When you swipe your card, you not only pay for your purchase, but you can also request cash back up to a certain amount. In most cases, this is simply billed as part of your purchase and, as a result, you will not assume any fees. You might also consider periodic withdrawals which involves withdrawing enough to cover your expenses for an extended period of time, say an entire month. Instead of making weekly withdrawals, you're only withdrawing enough to cover your expenses. Otherwise, it can be difficult to avoid the temptation to spend the money in your pocket.

Certificates of Deposit

These simple financial products are offered by banks and other financial institutions to provide consumers with an insured way of protecting their savings. CDs are unlike typical savings accounts as they are usually based on a fixed term and a fixed interest rate. The CD must be held until maturity when the principal and accrued interest can be withdrawn. Because your money is locked up for a period of time, anywhere from a month to several years, you can expect a slightly higher interest rate on CDs than on a typical savings account. Jumbo CDs offer even higher rates but require a minimum deposit of $100,000.

It is possible to withdraw a CD before maturity, but it will be subject to hefty fees.

Money Market Accounts

Money market accounts usually require a minimum balance but pay a higher rate of interest than typical savings accounts. This allows the account holder to avoid fees. The resulting structure is similar to a money market fund offered by brokerage houses.

Protecting Yourself with Insurance

Insurance is one of the most complicated and most often misunderstood financial concepts any of us will ever deal with. We buy it to cover us in case of unforeseen events and when these events do not surface, we ask ourselves whether we did the right thing by purchasing it. It's easy to understand the need for health insurance, but what about property, life, and auto? I've spent a decent amount on life insurance and, as far as I know, I'm still here. What about all the extra coverage on a car that I rarely drive? Do I really need it? Let's consider the different policies, what you absolutely need, and what you might scale back on. After all, it would be terrific to insure every aspect of your life, but the premiums to cover yourself alone could drive you into bankruptcy.

Insurance Quiz

- Do you like to ride motorcycles naked?

- Do you swim with open wounds in shark-infested waters?

- Do you fillet your own blowfish?

- Do you vacation in North Korea wearing a CIA T-shirt?

- If you answered yes to any of these questions, you probably don't care much about insurance and should skip this section.

Health Insurance

Here is the only thing you need to know about health insurance: Get it immediately. Whether it is federally mandated or not (I have a feeling I may be updating this section quite often for future editions), you need coverage. According to a Harvard University study, medical expenses are the number-one cause of bankruptcy and, while health care costs have reached stratospheric proportions, you can't afford to be without insurance. Sure, you might boast to your friends that you haven't been sick in years, but that doesn't mean you're immune to illness and, more importantly, made of titanium. A nasty fall, a fender bender, or a bad night of drinking can each lead to costly medical bills. Trust me on this one. Worse, I've seen friends and relatives come out of the hospital with seven-figure hospital bills. That's more than most people make in a lifetime, and one life-threatening illness can set you back a cool mill. I don't know about you, but I'd rather not spend the rest of my life making payments to the hospital. So, what next? If possible, get a job with a good medical benefits plan. This should include medical, medical prescription, dental, and eyesight coverage. When choosing the right plan, always consider the following:

Premium. This is the amount you pay each month. Whether you go to the doctor or not, you still pay. Make sure it's reasonable and, while it might seem excessive, understand just what you're getting. Usually, the higher the monthly premium, the lower the deductible.

Deductible. This is what you pay should you require a medical exam or medical treatment. This can be complex, so make sure you understand what you would spend on an emergency room visit as well as a major hospitalization.

Copay. This represents the amount you pay out-of-pocket for things like doctor visits or prescription drugs. It's usually a fixed-dollar amount you pay at the time of service.

Coinsurance. I love this one. It sounds good, almost like additional coverage. The reality, of course, is quite different. This represents the percentage of the service cost that you must pay.

Life Insurance

If you're a complete misanthrope and generally avoid every other human being on the planet, life insurance is probably not for you. However, if there are people you are close to, it makes sense to protect them financially in the event of your untimely passing. The different types of life insurance are outlined below:

Term. This is usually the most affordable type with one specific purpose: pay your beneficiaries in the event of your untimely passing. Terms can be as short as one year and as long as several decades. These policies sometimes require a review of your family's financial situation. Make sure you understand all rules and obligations associated with a policy and, by all means, comparison shop. No two policies are alike.

Whole life. Unlike term insurance, a whole-life policy offers guaranteed benefits and the premiums never change. Additionally, this policy will carry a cash value, meaning a portion of what you pay in premium is designated as value that you maintain. You can draw money from this value, which can create an effective investment vehicle. Additionally, the cash value will grow at a rate that can be as high as four percent. So, while you pay more in premiums for whole-life policies than term-life policies, the investment benefits may make sense for you.

Universal life. This type of policy will offer significant flexibility, allowing you to adjust your premiums and even decide how much is allocated toward the cash value vs. benefits. In other words, you decide how your premiums are allocated, which in turn affects your coverage.

Auto Insurance

Auto insurance really comes down to a few types of coverage that you must be aware of:

Bodily injury liability. This type of coverage is required in most states and covers you for injuries you cause someone else.

Personal injury protection. This will cover the driver and the passengers of the policyholder's car for treatment of injuries. I once heard of a guy who sprained his thumb while thumb wrestling another passenger. I can't say if that injury would be covered, but check your policy terms if you plan on engaging in extracurricular activities while in transit. And again, get health insurance if you like to thumb wrestle.

Property damage liability. Also required by most states, it will cover damage you cause to someone else's property.

Collision coverage. Usually an optional policy feature, collision insurance will cover damage sustained by your car in the event of a collision. If your car is held together by duct tape, you may want to skip collision insurance (but make sure you have personal injury protection!).

Comprehensive coverage. Also optional, comprehensive insurance should cover you for damage cause by noncollision-related events such as fire, theft, vandalism, bird droppings, meteor showers, angry exes, and so on.

Uninsured motorist coverage. A good thing to have as it covers you should you sustain injuries from a driver who isn't insured.

Homeowners

I'm a big fan of this type of insurance as you never really know what to expect as a homeowner. And, all too often, life's little surprises can become humongous expenses. Homeowners insurance provides financial protection for your home, its contents, and your valuable possessions. Many policies will offer a customization option, which is useful given that your home and possessions may be unique. At the very least, make sure you have enough coverage to pay for the cost of rebuilding your home. This could be more than the appraised value of your home so make sure you account for it. Also, outline specific items to be covered in your policy, such as jewelry and family heirlooms. The last thing you want to do is scramble to prove that your grandmother created the secret formula for Coca-Cola, which your cat just swallowed.

Renters

Far too many renters believe that they simply do not own enough property to justify the cost of renters insurance. Huge mistake. Renter's insurance covers just about everything you own, and the cost of a policy can be nominal. Imagine what happens if your apartment is burglarized. Your clothes, stereo, TV, bike, books, jewelry, computer, and furniture will likely be gone. Do you really want to spend the time and money to replace all of these items? For a few hundred dollars per year, you can financially protect yourself against theft, fire, flood, and so on. Many policies will protect you against personal liability. So, the next time you throw a bash and that unruly guest breaks his nose doing a keg stand, you can tell him to clean up the blood and have another beer—you're covered.

Disability

Disability insurance is an income supplement covering you in the event that you are unable to work. In other words, it's an income replacement that covers up to 75 percent of your income. Larger companies may provide this, but don't count on it. And if you work for a small company or are self-employed, you need to think seriously about this. I could spend pages listing why you may suddenly become unable to work, but I'll spare you. The point is, should an unfortunate chain of events keep you from gainful employment, disability insurance can be a good stress alleviator. The last thing you want to do when incapacitated is worry about who will pay your bills.

Chapter Lessons

- Risk free bank accounts will keep your money safe, but don't expect to grow wealth.

- Make sure you understand all fees when choosing a bank account.

- Consider protecting your home, possessions, and livelihood through insurance policies and always carry health insurance.

Financial Advisors

Who do I trust? Me!

—Tony Montana, *Scarface*

One of the best lessons in all of finance was voiced so eloquently by Al Pacino's iconic drug-lord character, Tony Montana. Too bad Tony's words of wisdom are lost in a barrage of bullets. I've taken his attitude toward nearly every business matter. I realize that there are smart people out there who do this type of thing for a living, but it pays to question the experts. Never lose sight of this and you just might save yourself a lot of pain and heartache. Just ask anyone who invested with Bernie Madoff.

Get 'er done!

—Larry the Cable Guy

You've learned everything about personal finance and, at this point, have realized one thing: Personal finance is boring. Well, it doesn't have to be, but if after learning about it, you still feel this way, there is no need to force yourself to devote your precious time to managing your resources. However, this is by no means an excuse to ignore your financial affairs. If you despise dealing with these things, neither this book nor any other can make you love them. However, you should at least recognize the importance of staying on top of your financial affairs and outsource them to the experts. These are the people you need in your back pocket.

In this chapter, we'll cover two topics:

- Three advisors you need
- What to look for in an advisor

Three Advisors You Need

Stockbrokers, Financial Planners, Money Managers

In case you didn't get the memo, the world has changed. Thanks to Charles Schwab and the Internet, the role of a stockbroker isn't what it used to be. Decades ago, if you wanted to buy or sell stock, you needed to go through a stockbroker. Nowadays, completing such transactions is as easy as turning on a computer, and it costs a fraction of what it used to. Stockbrokers do exist and, like any profession, you have your good ones and your not-so-good ones. If you decide to use a stockbroker for your financial transactions, make sure you choose one with a good reputation, a decent client list, and reasonable fees. Otherwise, you could find yourself simply paying too much for something you could have done yourself.

Financial planners make money by charging you an hourly fee, a transaction fee, a management fee, or some combination of these three. If possible, avoid the transaction-fee structure as this creates incentives for the financial planner to push high-commission-paying products and securities your way. Hourly fees can be hit-or-miss given that you don't always keep track of the amount of time the financial planners are putting into managing your account. If you can handle the management fees, they will likely give you the most return on your investment.

Look for professionals who carry the credential of certified financial planner (CFP). While this alone doesn't mean they're going to score you triple-digit gains on your stock portfolio, at least you can breathe easy knowing they are licensed and regulated. These guys will not only give you advice on how to save but how to invest as well. Think of them as a one-stop shop for budgeting and growth. Some will specialize in particular areas, such as retirement planning, or offer expertise on achieving a financial goal, such as buying a home.

Financial managers tend to do everything from invest your money to help you plan for retirement. Think of them as a one-stop shop for your financial needs and their fees usually reflect that. They come with all kinds of neat credentials but, ultimately, you want someone with good experience and a strong reputation. They will typically charge a fee based on your portfolio size, but the fee should include advisory services as well as transaction fees. If you have $100,000 under management, paying $1,000 per year may not be so bad if your financial planner gives sound advice, boosts your returns, and does dozens of transactions each year.

Ask for references and, ultimately, make sure you're comfortable dealing with the CFP you choose because, after all, your future rests in this person's hands. Don't be afraid to shop around for a financial planner and, if you find one you like, there is nothing wrong with trying things out for, say, three months. This is your money and you have every right to test the waters.

Advantages

Free or low-cost financial research. The cost of financial research can reach thousands of dollars per month. Many financial advisors will offer access to reports free of charge.

Commission-free products. Many advisors will allow unlimited trades without commission.

Timely execution of trades. Having a professional handle your investment activities can mean acting on opportunities even when you're not available.

Strategic planning to cover most of your financial goals. Working with a trained professional will enable you to meet periodically to discuss short-term and long-term goals.

Access to new financial products and offerings. This can be one of the best advantages of all. Nothing wrong with a little preferential treatment.

Disadvantages

Fees. Fees can run upward of one percent of your total portfolio value, and additional fees can be added to individual transactions. Know what you're getting yourself into.

Biases. These guys may have a tendency to push their own products, especially if they're part of a larger financial institution active in the underwriting process.

Upselling. The name of the game is to sell, so financial planners may try to sell you more than you need.

Insurance Broker

These guys can pester you like crazy, but I will say, the ones I have used have found me the best rates on home, auto, and health insurance. Additionally, if I need any information or have any questions, they are usually pretty helpful.

For purposes of simplicity and keeping your finances organized, I suggest finding one good broker to handle all of your needs. They can find multi-policy discounts for you and serve as a one-stop shop for any of your informational needs. Trust me on this because insurance is the kind of thing you can forget you have until you really need it. Next time you back your car into your garage door, it's nice to know that one call will get you your homeowners insurance information for the garage door, your auto insurance information for your bumper, and your health insurance information for your whiplash. And if you're prone to backing up moving vehicles into stationary objects, they might even refer you to a driving school.

Advantages

Best rates. Insurance brokers are plugged in and can theoretically find you the best rates available.

Counseling. They can advise you on what types of policies make sense for you.

Bundling. They can offer better rates by combining policies.

Disadvantages

Commissions. You can bet they are getting a fee from each policy they sell, so you might fare better buying your policy direct from the provider.

Bias. They may steer you to a higher-premium policy.

Upselling. They may try to convince you to add on features to your policy that you don't really need.

Accountant

Depending on the complexity of your professional life, you should consider using an accountant. If you have one job and few investments, you can probably just use an accounting service once a year to do your taxes. This will run you at least $100, but if it saves you a day of fumbling through online tax forms, it might be worth it. More importantly, if you have jobs, a side business, or multiple investment properties; you perform in a circus that travels the world and performs on cruise ships; you recently hired a sidekick from another country for your acrobatic routines and pay her in local currency; you wear a leotard for your act and it must be dry-cleaned every day; you invest your circus wages in diamond mines in Equatorial Guinea … get a good accountant and, come to think of it, a decent lawyer. OK, so most of us don't fall into this category, but as your finances become more complicated, it might help to have a good accountant.

Advantages

Time. Accountants can save you a ton of time, especially at tax time.

Timely response. They can handle your correspondence with the government when issues arise and often stay ahead of deadlines.

Expertise. When it comes to accounting matters, most of us are prone to mistakes. Fortunately, these guys get paid to avoid mistakes so hopefully that saves you time and money.

Disadvantages

Cost. Most accountants bill hourly, so these fees can really add up.

Complications. Accountants sometimes take a simple situation and make it more complicated. Not to say they're doing anything wrong, but good luck trying to understand the matter.

Loss of freedom. Accounting is at the heart of personal finance. If you outsource these matters, you run the risk of losing control of your financial status.

What to Look For in an Advisor

I apply the same rules to choosing an advisor as I do to dating.

Appearance. Clean and well-groomed is a must. If they don't take care of themselves, how are they going to take care of your financial matters? Sure, there are exceptions, but I don't want to take the chance.

Accessibility. Do they return calls promptly? If not, it might be time to move on to another one.

Openness. If they are not telling you what they are up to regarding your financial matters, you might have a problem. Just ask anyone who invested with Mr. Madoff.

Reputation. Do they have a bad reputation? Case closed.

Chapter Lessons

- If you are too busy to manage your financial affairs, seek out others to help and be willing to pay for their services.

- Make sure you research the background and reputation of any financial advisor.

- No matter how good an advisor seems, always trust your instincts.

Conclusion

Congratulations! You made it. While you may not be quite ready to launch your own line of wealth-building DVDs or offer money-saving tips on late night TV, you have hopefully developed an appreciation for responsible personal finance. The most important thing to remember is that smart financial decisions lead to personal freedom. Making the right choices with your pocketbook will help you live the kind of life you have always dreamed of. Make the wrong choices and you may end up talking to the banks more than your family.

My advice to you going forward is this: Don't obsess over financial matters. Live your life to the fullest; even make sure you splurge at times. However, make sure your indulgences do not compromise your future. If your shoe collection forces you to work nights in a bar, perhaps it's time to consider whether it's worth it. On the other hand, if a couple of nice pairs make you happy and your career isn't affected by them, no problem. There's no magic formula here. Just make sure you can justify the price. And price isn't just the price tag. It's everything you pay in terms of time and effort.

To reach the goal of financial freedom, you must ensure that your money is working for you. This requires careful attention to saving and investing. Make the wrong choices and you will be working for the rest of your life or, worse, working for the banks (and paying them rather than the other way around).

Going forward, you should reread this book from time to time. Better yet, grab yourself a new copy periodically (and help the author achieve his financial freedom). Managing your finances the smart way does not need to be a challenge. Indeed, it takes practice but once you get the hang of it, you'll find it comes naturally and you'll start to enjoy the benefits that come with it. Best of luck!

I

Index

CPSIA information can be obtained at www.ICGtesting.com
Printed in the USA
LVOW051955220113

316782LV00004B/492/P